"For years Jane Kinderlehrer has conned her husband and children into eating a high-protein, low-fat diet of foods loaded with vitamins and minerals of every description. And she's saved money too. 'It takes conviction, cunning and a talent for trickery,' Jane says, 'but you can raise a healthy family in the midst of pollution.'"
—Robert Rodale, *The Detroit News*

"Mrs. Kinderlehrer, who is a senior editor on *Prevention*, has a suggestion for anyone who wants to begin eating more healthfully and doesn't know quite where to start."
—Susan Rogers, *New York Post*

"This isn't just another health food book. It's fun. Jane has been with Rodale Press for a number of years (J. I. Rodale, the founder of the first organic farm in the U. S.) and knows her stuff inside and out. . . . Few of us, however, can make the switch from cheeseburgers and french fries to brown rice and bean sprouts. Jane Kinderlehrer makes it as painless as possible."
—Cheri Gay, *Detroit Free Press*

". . . we will see the results of sneaky organic cookery almost immediately in dispositions and school performance, and over a longer term in dental check-ups and fewer doctor's visits. . . . A good cook book . . . illuminating. . . ."
—*Let's Live*

"This book is a delight to read and sensible to heed. It should be a kitchen 'bible.'"
—Palm Springs, *Call Enterprise & Herald American*

Confessions of a Sneaky Organic Cook

or
How to Make Your Family Healthy When They're Not Looking!

Jane Kinderlehrer

Illustrations by JOSEPH J. CHARNOSKI

A SIGNET BOOK from
NEW AMERICAN LIBRARY
TIMES MIRROR

SIGNET, SIGNET CLASSICS, MENTOR, PLUME AND MERIDIAN BOOKS
are published by The New American Library, Inc.,
1301 Avenue of the Americas, New York, New York 10019

FIRST PRINTING, JUNE, 1972

8 9 10 11 12 13

Dedicated to

Every mother who yearns to see the glow of health
on the faces of her loved ones.

ACKNOWLEDGMENTS

The author wishes to express her thanks to all those who needled, encouraged, inspired and by other sundry and devious means helped get this book to the bookstore and to you.

Special thanks to Charles Gerras, my editor, who makes every problem a challenge to grow on and who, from his winged wheelchair, lives life more joyfully and more abundantly than anyone I know.

To Harald Taub, Jerry Goldstein and Glenn Johns for their tender loving care while this book was incubating.

To Carolyn Lichtman for her continuous encouragement and great recipes.

To Anna Wieder for her constant guidance and help testing recipes.

To Joan Bingham, Irene Somishka and Carol Bachman for editorial assistance.

To Rose Kinderlehrer who first introduced me to wheat germ.

And very special thanks to my kind husband and lovely children who inspired me to become a sneaky cook.

Contents

Chapter

I   Why Be Sneaky? 11

II   Don't Force It—Sneak It 15

III   How to Have Fresh, Organic Enzyme-Rich Vegetables, Winter or Summer, Without Going to Market 20

IV   Enlist Your Butcher's Cooperation 25

V   If You're Eating For Two 28

VI   Make Your *Own* Baby Food 34

VII   Lollipops—Reward or Punishment? 40

VIII   Teens Need More Nutrition and Are Getting Less 48

IX   How to Take the Blue Out of Monday ... 54

X   When Happiness Was a Pocketful of Polly Seeds 71

XI   Get Smart—Use Brains 77

XII   Change Your Sex Life Without Changing Partners 80

XIII   Darling, Your Deficiencies are Showing .. 89

XIV   Change Your Snacks and Save Your Heart 100

XV   Have a Healthful Party and Make it a Smash! 104

XVI   How to Lose Weight—and Feel Great—Without Hardly Dieting 112

XVII   Who's Afraid of a Sneaky Cook? 121

Index 195

Chapter I

Why Be Sneaky?

The very first thing you do when you get your hands on this book is—*read it in private*. Then, put a plain jacket on it—preferably washable—and HIDE it carefully. Don't let the children get even a peek at it or the jig is up. I am about to sharewith you some top-secret pointers on how to give your family more zip, zest and zingo—*when they're not looking*.

But, why be sneaky about it? Why the James Bond 007 intrigue? Why not straight from the shelf and into the pot? Why? I'll tell you why. Because, at certain stages of their growth and development (like from toddlers through teens and right up to the coronary stage) anything that smacks of "health" is considered square, for the birds, or, when they get sophisticated, "faddist."

Sneaky cookery is the art of incorporating into every dish the food values, the vitamins and minerals and enzymes which would have been there in the first place if

11

the food had not been processed, devitalized and loaded with additives and thus stripped of much of its nutritive value.

At this point, you might just be thinking: "I've got a doctor, he's a great guy, I love him. Why do I need sneaky cooking?"

Just for the fun of it, take a look at your doctor's last statement. What are you billed for—Tony's tonsillitis, Susie's earache, Daddy's low back syndrome with possible herniated disc, Mamma's cystitis, Grandma's arthritis? Is there a single item on that statement for *promoting good health,* for *preventing colds and complications,* for *preventing a coronary,* for *Susie's marvelous complexion,* for *the wonderful way you want to feel?*

When you come right down to it, you don't engage your doctor to keep you in good health, do you? You hire him to make you feel better—*after you get sick.*

The ancient Chinese had a great system. They hired their doctors to keep them well. As soon as they got sick, the doctor went off the payroll. Until we get around to adopting the way of the ancient Chinese, it is up to us—the mothers, kitchen wizards, women of valor whose price is far beyond rubies—it is up to us to look well to the ways of our households, that our loved ones might enjoy good health and achieve their greatest potential.

Knowing what to feed your family is not enough. Getting them to eat it is the real challenge.

In this book we shall cover both aspects—not only what your loved ones need for optimum good health, but how to get it into them without any fights or fuss. That's where sneaky cookery comes in. Since I've been practicing sneaky cookery, all sorts of wonderful things have been happening. For instance, before sneaky cookery we used to have the doctor at least once a month. Now I can't even remember his phone number!

The children come home from their dental check-ups with big "Look, Mom, no cavities" grins; and I mean *NO* cavities—not just one; their dispositions and mine are much sunnier and they're all doing much better in school. I have a funny, teasing feeling that the key to many of our unexplained ailments is in the hand of our kitchen alchemists —that every chief cook and bottle washer wields much more power than she is aware of. Sneaky cookery can be your valuable ally in fighting the good fight.

Here's a good sneaky trick to get you started. Just before dinner when the children are ravenous and will eat anything that doesn't eat them first, put out a large tray full of celery sticks, carrot sticks, raw turnip slices, pepper rings, radishes and any other vegetables in season. Deftly remove all the pretzels, potato chips, corn curls and candies and throw them to the birds.

Once you have taken this step, you are on your way—follow through.

How to have a Healthful Kitchen—(No harmful things and all of the essentials)

The "Good-Nutrition" cook rids her pantry of these foods:

1. Bleached white flour
2. Refined sugar
3. All shortenings that are solid at room temperature
4. White rice
5. Maraschino cherries (they're loaded with harmful preservatives)
6. Any product loaded with BHA or BHT (freshness preservers)
7. Fruits canned with sugar syrup (There are some that are not)
8. All synthetic sweeteners and products sweetened with them (saccharin as well as cyclamates)
9. All sugared dry cereals
10. Hydrogenated peanut butters (use the natural)
11. All candy made with refined sugar
12. Commercial breads that are loaded with emulsifiers and preservatives
13. Refined table salt

The "Good-Nutrition" cook keeps on her pantry shelf:

1. Raw honey
2. Raw sugar
3. Date sugar
4. Soy flour
5. Whole wheat flour (stone ground)
6. Carob flour (chocolate substitute)
7. Wheat germ (in the refrigerator)
8. Wheat germ oil (in the refrigerator)
9. Soy and sesame oils (cold pressed) in the refrigerator
10. Nutritional yeast (sometimes called brewer's yeast)
11. Sesame seeds (unhulled)
12. Sunflower seeds (raw)
13. Pumpkin seeds
14. Kelp (as a salt substitute)
15. Sea salt
16. Unsweetened coconut

17.   Seeds for sprouting (wheat, rye, oat, mung beans, soy
      beans, alfalfa, etc.)
18.   Raw nuts

Most of these foods are not yet available in supermarkets. You can find them in practically all health-food
stores. If you've never been in one, you should go. You
meet the nicest people in health-food stores.

What Kind of Pots Does She Use?

I use stainless steel for top of stove use and pyro-ceram
for oven use. I do not use aluminum because aluminum
leaches into the food. I will not use Teflon because, at high
temperatures, Teflon releases a deadly gas. True, these high
temperatures are not necessary for ordinary cooking. But
you know as well as I that there are times when you turn
on the light under an empty pan in preparation for filling
it, the telephone rings or the dog wants to go out or the
baby screams—and the pot is forgotten until the pan is
overheated and deadly chemicals are released.

Chapter II

Don't Force It—Sneak It

Before you embark on the exciting and daring venture of Sneaky Cookery, observe these cardinal rules.

1. Practice all tricks with a very light touch. Play it cool.
2. Always be prepared to beat a fast retreat—but never, no never, reveal your strategy. Take the Fifth.
3. Never let your nutritional zeal overwhelm your sense of humor. Don't be grim.

Now, let's get started. You have some dry skim milk, or some soy powder? Good. So take a tablespoon, just one, mind you, and blend it carefully with a little milk from the bottle. Blend it until absolutely smooth in order to avoid telltale lumps. Now put it back in the bottle and recap. If there is no comment from the peanut gallery after a week of this milk, try adding two tablespoons, and then three, until you can safely add one-third of a cup to a quart of milk. In "Let's Have Healthy Children" Adelle Davis suggests a half-cup of dried skim milk to 2 cups of fresh milk. I never got that far.

Now, if at any time during the progression, there is any comment on the funny taste of the milk, *make like Sarah Bernhardt*. Open your eyes wide in dismay, taste the milk very thoughtfully and then AGREE. "You are absolutely right—this milk does have a strange taste. I'm going to take this up with the milk man. Those cows must have been grazing in the garlic grass again, and the milk got past the milk smeller at the dairy. Yes, of course they have a milk smeller. That's what he does all day—smells the milk as the farmers bring it in. Say, wouldn't he be a great one for 'What's My Line?' They'd never guess." Now, get another bottle of milk out, one that hasn't been so ambitiously spiked, and say, "Let's try this one—maybe it comes from a more conservative cow."

If you pass this milestone, you're well on your way to an advanced degree in Sneaky Cookery. Now start decreasing the amount of dry milk until you find the best tolerance level—and stay there. Our children got so accustomed to the taste of spiked milk that when, on occasions, they had milk outside, they would say—"This milk tastes funny—must be from a cow that went mooching in the garlic grass."

Now, when you make puddings, add the powdered milk to the dry mix before you add the milk—about two tablespoons to the package. Add powdered milk to baked goods, creamed soups, pancakes, muffins, casseroles, kugels, cakes and cookies. This one little sneaky device will give your family more zip because they'll be getting more protein, more calcium and several important vitamins—most notably, B_2 (riboflavin) which plays an important role in mental health, and in the health of the skin, eyes, liver and heart. In these foods, the taste is not detectable. Not even our pickiest eater has ever remarked about their peculiar flavor. Yet I always enrich them with powdered milk.

Remember, when your children complain of growing pains or menstrual cramps, they are often signaling a need for more calcium. If you have nothing on the menu at these times into which you can get some powdered milk, try tempting them with delicious milk shakes fortified with extra powdered milk. Eliminate the syrup. Add some natural vanilla or fresh or frozen fruit instead. They don't need the sugar. Fruit has a natural sweetness.

If you are trying to lose weight, don't overlook your own needs for calcium and for fats. Contrary to popular conception, it is not too much calcium which causes deposits. It is poor utilization or absorption. In order for calcium to be absorbed into the blood stream, you must have an adequate amount of vitamin C, vitamin D, and of unsaturated fats. Keep this in mind or your dieting can lead to wrinkles and gall bladder troubles. Remember, too, when calcium is under-supplied, nerves become tense and you get grouchy.

As a change from certified raw milk, I frequently serve soy milk (great if your child is among those who are allergic to cow's milk).

You can make soy milk from soy powder (directions come with it) or from soy beans.

Soy Bean Milk

Wash 1 cup soy beans and soak overnight in plenty of water. Put beans and 3 cups of water in the blender and whiz until pulpy. Discard the soak water or use it for your house plants.

Put the blended mixture into a large stainless steel kettle and simmer gently for 15 minutes. Strain through a very fine sieve or stout cloth.

Refrigerate the milk until used. If you don't have a blender, drain the beans and grind through a food chopper, add the water and simmer and strain (the same as with the blended mixture).

There are some foods which, when used liberally, provide you with a broad spectrum of almost all the vitamins, minerals, and enzymes you need to keep that wonderful machine of yours in top-top shape. I almost hesitate to tell you all the terrific dividends that accrue when you use them because you might get carried away and overdo. You might tend to push it too hard or show your chagrin when the children turn up their noses. That sort of approach just doesn't work. It tends to divide your family into two opposing camps—and who wins? You just can't lick a closed-mouth strike. That's why my guiding principle is *"Don't Force it—Sneak it."*

It's unfortunate that one of these foods should be called what it is because right away the uninitiated, who need it most, think it creeps. In this instance the word "germ" means heart or essence of life—and wheat germ is full of life-giving nutrients that, before flour was refined, made bread the staff of life.

Unless you are using whole-wheat flour, the wheat germ has been removed from the flour in your canister. It's been removed from your bread, cakes, crackers, cookies, bagels, noodles, and dry cereals. You know why? Because wheat germ supports life. Therefore, it spoils more readily. Without the wheat germ, flour has longer staying qualities, longer shelf life, and can be shipped more readily all over the world. It is commercially expedient to remove the wheat germ from the flour.

Well, what about enriched flour, enriched bread, enriched cereals? That word "enriched" has been pulling the wool over our eyes and leading us down the path to deficiencies for too many years. Look at it this way. If someone stole your wallet with $200 in it, your favorite snapshots, credit cards, and driver's license, and returned your emptied wallet, license, and 20 cents for car fare to you, would you consider yourself enriched? There are 33 nutrients in the wheat germ that have been removed from the flour and every one of them is essential to the assembly line that keeps your body running on all cylinders. In the so-called "enrichment" process, only three of these nutrients are put back—and these in only one-third of the original amount, and in a synthetic form which is not well utilized.

The irony of this "enrichment" program is that so many of the diseases, which afflict young and old alike, are the result of metabolic disturbances caused by deficiencies of the very vitamins, minerals, and enzymes that are in the wheat germ that was removed from the flour.

How do you fight City Hall? How do you get the wheat germ into your family's diet? Since it's a natural component of flour, I use it whenever I use flour. And if you rarely use flour because of the convenience of the commercial packaged mixes, try adding wheat germ to the mix before you add the egg and liquid. I like to bake cakes from "scratch," so to speak but, if I'm having guests and am rushed for time, I might use a mix and spike it generously with wheat germ. The trick here is to run the wheat germ through the blender for a minute. This reduces it to a finer consistency so eagle eyes can't detect it.

It's the funniest thing but invariably one of my guests, usually a male, will say as he reaches for a second helping, "You can't fool me—this cake wasn't made from a mix—it has that ole time flavor that just doesn't come in a box." I just make like Mona Lisa and smile—but never tell. It's better they shouldn't know how healthy they're getting.

If your children will take wheat germ with their cereal or instead of it, you've got it made. If you can't get them to take it, take it yourself. You'll have that much more of the zip you need to deal with their *michigasim*. (That's Yiddish for crazy notions.)

Know how I got my children to take wheat germ in their cereal? I changed the label on the jar. After all, if you've been cramming for exams, and your nerves are on edge, can you resist "Anti-Stupid Molecules" or "High I.Q. Granules"? Such a label is worth a thousand words. If you want to win young boys over, label the jar "Muscle Power" or "Batman Glow." Girls, whether they're playing with toys or boys, enjoy helping themselves to "Complexion Beauty." Go creative! Capitalize on their current interest or pander to their passion of the moment—but *Don't Force!*

Chapter III

How to Have Fresh, Organic Enzyme-Rich Vegetables, Winter or Summer, Without Going to Market

What is it that rivals meat for protein, has more vitamin C than tomatoes, supplies practically all the nutrients your body needs, has no waste at all in preparation, requires little or no fuel to prepare, can be used on land or sea, or in snow-bound villages, and can be produced almost like magic as needed?

Give up?

The answer is SPROUTS.

If you, like most of us, are seeking a source of fresh unsprayed, vitamin-rich vegetables for every day of the year, without busting your budget and with hardly a visit to the market, you can do it very simply, by growing sprouts. You don't need a garden plot, a backyard or even a window box. You can grow vitamin-protein-enzyme-rich sprouts, free of insects, free of insecticides and free of artificial fertilizers on your windowsill, on your table, on the edge of your sink, or under your sink!

A sprouting grain is unique. It is the only foodstuff which we can consume humanely while the life force is still vibrant. A seed that is sprouting has within its kernel the essence of life—it is still steeped in self-creation and produces in abundance all life-giving elements.

Give the seed proper conditions and it will reward you in countless ways. It will almost explode with vital life force. A tiny little sprout appears. The sprout grows, vitamins, minerals and enzymes are quickly formed. Its nutritional content skyrockets almost overnight.

The most spectacular rise is in vitamin C. While sprouting, soybeans undergo a 553% increase in vitamin C. Imagine! Where can you get that kind of interest on your investment? The 11 milligrams of C in 100 grams of whole oats become 42 milligrams after five days of sprouting.

Other vitamins, too, make spectacular jumps. B_2 increases by 1350% in oats after five days of germination. Folic acid rises from 28 parts in dry wheat to 106 parts in the sprouted grain. Niacin content of Mung beans quadruples in value. The riboflavin content of corn, barley and wheat quadruples. Pyridoxine and pantothenic acid (expensive vitamins usually short changed in synthetic formulations) triple in the sprouts. The fat soluble vitamins A, E and K also soar in sprouts.

Some seeds develop complete protein patterns capable of sustaining life, with the fats and carbohydrates, the calcium, iron, phosphorus, potassium and other minerals the seed contains. The carbohydrate content is very low which makes sprouts practically a wonder food for weight watchers.

Every good nutrition housewife should make it her business to know the delight of growing some of these miracle foods that can be raised in any climate, planted any day of the year. They can travel with you on vacations; they are inexpensive, require no soil or thought to weather conditions and provide a marvelous way to show children the secret of seeds. At the same time, they help them to learn a good lesson in nutrition.

Here is an easy way to grow the alfalfa seed which is so rich in Vitamin K, the blood clotting vitamin, plus the valuable nutrient chlorophyll.

Put one tablespoon of alfalfa seed in a pint jar. Fill the jar half full of tepid water, then let stand overnight. Next morning, drain this water off into a glass or jar, to be mixed with fruit juice or used in soup stock. It contains valuable vitamins and minerals.

Now rinse the seed with fresh water—not cold and not hot, just lukewarm. You can use a tea strainer for this or you can simply cover the mouth of the jar with two thicknesses of cheesecloth and secure it with a rubber band. After rinsing the seeds, turn the jar upside down or tilt it slightly so that any moisture that is left can escape but the seeds still get a source of oxygen. Some people use netting or a circle of wire mesh to fit into the jar's top ring.

Rinse the seeds this way two or three times each day and by the second day you will see the white roots starting to push out. Be sure to shake the seeds apart each time you rinse them so that they will not grow into a tight mat. Use a fork to stir them if necessary, but be gentle so that you do not break any.

When the small leaves turn a bright green on about the fourth day, then you know they are rich in cholrophyll and ready to enjoy. Eat the whole sprout—the old seed, shell, the tiny root, the stem, the leaves, everything in the jar.

How do you eat them? Let me count the ways. Add them to soups, to salads, to chopped meat dishes or enjoy them topped with a little yogurt and a few sunflower seeds. Any sandwich is enriched, and enhanced, by adding alfalfa sprouts instead of the usual lettuce.

During World War II, when food shortages threatened the nation's health, Governor Dewey of New York called together his food experts and said in effect: "Gentlemen, I want you to find a food that can be grown quickly and easily, will supply all possible nourishment and will continue to be plentiful no matter what other foods may be scarce."

The food researchers came up with the soybean. There are many surprises for most people in the soybean, Dr. McCay (School of Nutrition, Cornell University) pointed out. "One is that ordinary field variety of soybeans are ready for the dinner table after they are sprouted, or they can be cooked ready to eat in 10 minutes. Another surprise is that sprouted beans can prevent scurvy due to the formation of Vitamin C while the bean is sprouting. Furthermore sprouted soybeans are not likely to produce intestinal gases."

Soybeans have a very chewy texture—crisp and waxy, like the peanut. They will not get mushy like dried beans do, even after long cooking. Hence they need be cooked only long enough to remove the raw bean flavor—usually 10 minutes is sufficient.

Soybean sprouts can be sautéed lightly and served as a hot vegetable. Use very little oil. The soybean has its own built-in supply. Try this method: Lightly brown some sliced onion, add the bean sprouts and a very small amount of water. Cook for about 10 minutes.

The crispy texture of the bean sprout makes it a welcome addition to raw vegetable salads.

The Chinese add chopped sprouts with soy sauce to scrambled eggs and omelets. They call it egg foo yung.

The sprouts served with your Chinese dinner are mung beans. You can have a continuous supply of these crisp delicious sprouts by following pretty much the same directions as those given for alfalfa. Put one-third cup in a jar and cover with water. Mung beans should soak 8 hours or overnight. (If you see bubbles forming in the water, you have soaked them too long. Wash them well, until there is no longer any odor of fermentation, and proceed.) Place soaked beans in a widemouthed quart jar. Cover top with nylon net or a double layer of cheese cloth and secure with a rubber band. Place the jar in a bowl or a pie plate and put it in a warm, dark place. If you have a cupboard under your sink, that is the perfect place for it. It's kept comfortably warm by the hot water pipe. The only trouble is you're apt to forget that they're there and neglect to rinse them. Make a little reminder card "Rinse Sprouts" and place it on the edge of your sink. Rinse them at least twice a day.

Don't limit your sprouting creativity to one or two varieties. Be bold; experiment with unhulled sesame, sunflower, millet, chia, radish, clover, parsley, mustard, fenugreek, wheat, rye, oats, corn, barley, lentils, green peas, lima beans, chick peas, marrow beans, cranberry beans, fava beans.

Do not overlook the small seeds. The smaller they are, the more vital they are. Sesame, alfalfa and chia seeds are good examples.

Points to remember: be sure to get only certified organically grown seeds, or seeds you have grown organically yourself. Commercial seeds are frequently treated with chemicals—wheat seed, for instance is usually doused with mercury poisons to kill rust and smut disease organisms, and other grains are treated to prevent weevil infestation in storage.

Catharyn Elwood, author of "Feel Like a Million" (Devlin-Adair) makes these suggestions on when to use your sprouts:

"Wheat sprouts are most delicious when the sprout is the same length as the seed.
"Mung bean sprouts are best when 1½ to 3 inches long.
"Alfalfa sprouts are best when the little green leaves are well developed.
"Pea and soybean sprouts are good short or long.
"Sunflower seed sprouts are best when no longer than the seed. If longer they develop a strange sting in the throat after eating."

Keep jars of sprouts in the refrigerator for munching. They make very satisfying snacks. But don't stop there. Use them on salads. Drop them into soups just before serving. Rye sprouts taste a lot like wild rice. Try adding a handful to your brown rice dishes. Here is a great recipe to get you started using your soybean sprouts.

Sprouted Soybean Curry

1 medium onion	2 tablespoons soy flour
1 medium apple	1 teaspoon curry powder
2 to 4 stalks celery	1 teaspoon sea salt
2 tablespoons oil	⅛ teaspoon paprika
1½ cups meat stock or tomato juice	½ cup raisins, seedless
	3 cups sprouted soybeans

Cut onion, apple and celery up fine. Lightly brown in the hot oil. Add stock or tomato juice. Mix flour, curry powder, salt and paprika together and make a paste with a small amount of water. Stir paste into vegetable mixture thoroughly. Add ½ cup raisins. Add sprouted soybeans. Let simmer 15 minutes.

Chapter IV

Enlist Your Butcher's Cooperation

When it comes to sneaky cookery, your butcher can be your best friend. Mine has been in cahoots with me for years. When I order my "hamburger" mixture, he knows what I mean. If he didn't, I would have great difficulty placing my order over the phone. My children have big ears.

You see, the meats that are most important to the health of your family are the organ meats—liver, kidney, brain, spleen, thymus, heart and lung. They are also the best buys because there is so little demand for them. You can just imagine what kind of a closed-mouth strike you'd have around your table if you tried serving these foods frequently—unless you can serve them by some other name and texture. It isn't just the emotional impact of these foods which make them low beefs on the totem pole. They have a texture which is different and does not appeal to everybody.

Vive La Difference

What kind of meat can you serve frequently without that "Oh, this again," rejoinder? Hamburger. Not just patties in buns—patties without buns with a tomato sauce; rice and meat sauce, chow mein, stuffed peppers, stuffed cabbage, kreplach, meat loaf. You could serve it every night in a different guise and they wouldn't complain. So—hamburger is the natural medium for your organ meats. That's right. Your butcher grinds up heart, lungs, kidney or whatever you wish to conceal with your round or chuck. My standing order is two pounds of chuck, one pound of heart, one pound of lung—all ground together. That gives me four pounds of wonderfully nutritious meat at half the price— if you're economy minded.

My butcher, who, incidentally, now uses this mixture for his own family and can't thank me enough for the idea, gives me valiant service. He wraps the meat for the freezer in one-pound packages so that it's always ready to go into one of my frequently-served chopped-meat recipes. It is a juicy, tasty mixture which the children love—and so do their friends who come to dinner. When one of them, who is now in college, was invited to come to dinner during semester break he said, "May I come the night you're having hamburgers? I don't know what your secret is, but will you please give it to my wife when I get hitched?"

This is my children's favorite dish.

Rice and Meat Sauce

In the morning, take a package of ground meat, heart-lung mixture, from the freezer. Let it thaw in the refrigerator.

Brown two big chopped onions, three stalks of celery, some green pepper and parsley, in oil or chicken fat. (Use the celery tops, too.) When the vegetables are limp, add the defrosted meat. If it's still a little frozen, don't worry. It will soften in the pan. Mix with a fork to separate the particles of meat until they are all partially cooked (this takes about five minutes). Now add a cup of tomato sauce and a heaping tablespoon of brewer's yeast. About a tablespoon of barbecue sauce gives this mixture a nice piquancy that my children enjoy.

Serve this mixture on top of brown rice. Brown rice is

loaded with good B vitamins and vitamin E and has six times as much protein as white rice. Once you've tasted it, you'll enjoy its nutty flavor so much you won't go back to white. It's no more trouble to prepare either—just cooks a little longer.

Chapter V

If You're Eating for Two

Mrs. G., the nice motherly woman who is always handing out cookies to the neighborhood children, has been pregnant five times—but she has never had a baby. Each pregnancy was complicated by extreme nausea, toxemia and termination by spontaneous abortion. Mrs. G. says sadly that her fate has been ordained by Heaven.

Many women, when they become pregnant, leave it to Heaven to see them through to safe harbor. But Heaven helps those women who know and practice the rules of good nutrition.

Pregnancy can be the most beautiful and happy time in a woman's life—or it can be miserable and tragic. The big difference lies in you—more specifically in what you eat.

Is it the hand of fate, for instance, which directs one

woman to repeatedly lose her babies through miscarriage or spontaneous abortion? It is not fate at all, but very likely lack of some essential nutrient. Women who habitually abort have been helped tremendously to carry their babies to full term merely by adding bioflavonoids and vitamin C to their daily nutrients.

In few areas, tragically, is there so much lack of knowledge. What does constitute a good diet during pregnancy? What vitamins, for instance, can actually go to bat to guard you against the complications of pregnancy? What can you eat that will provide your unborn child with every possible chance to survive without physical or mental defects?

Many obstetricians believe they know, or claim to know, just what a pregnant woman should eat. Their opinions are based largely on guesswork or on their own necessarily limited range of individual experience. Few busy obstetricians have the time to keep up with the impressive number of well-designed and carefully executed investigations that reveal the important therapeutic relationships between diet and obstetrical complications.

In collating all these studies in a clear, concise, readable style, Dr. E. Cheraskin, head of the Department of Oral Medicine at the University of Alabama, made available for the first time a thorough statistical study, that moves the medical profession far closer to being able to pinpoint precisely what a pregnant woman should eat and why.

There were, for instance, 175,000 deaths in 1958 in the United States due to fetal fatality, stillbirth or neonatal mortality (deaths occurring close to the time of birth). Dr. Cheraskin and his collaborators conclude that more than half of these deaths could have been prevented with the application of present knowledge.

Rather exciting, Dr. Cheraskin says, is finding a reduction in the stillborn and neonatal death rate from erythroblastosis fetalis through vitamin C and the bioflavonids. It is especially exciting in view of the fact that this disorder, a result of Rh incompatibility, is regarded as genetic in origin and because bioflavonoids are seldom included in prenatal supplements.

Bioflavonoids are natural food substances found largely in the white membranes of citrus fruits and green peppers. They are non-toxic, therefore can do no harm even in large quantity, and are inexpensive as natural food supplements. Those who bruise easily, or have frequent nosebleeds, would do well to strengthen their capillary walls by increasing their intake of bioflavonoids. Every pregnant woman, whether she has an Rh problem or not, should certainly see to it that her diet is well fortified with ample bioflavonoids and vitamin C.

To get lots of bioflavonoids in your diet, score your grapefruit close to the outer skin and eat the connecting membranes. Eat your oranges whole—not juiced. If you can get some organically grown citrus fruit, use every bit of it. Peel the outer skin with a vegetable parer. Let these slivers dry—in the sun if possible. If this is not possible, just leave them on the back of the stove for a day or two. When they are dry and brittle, crumble them fine and use as a wonderful flavoring in cookies, cakes, on applesauce or cranberry sauce and in juices. Grapes are a good source of bioflavonoids. Perhaps your best source is rose hips. Use rose hip powder lavishly and make rose hip soup a staple of your diet.

Many women, before they ever don a maternity dress, have some experience with "morning sickness." It is often the first clue to start knitting little things. But is this nausea necessary? It will come as welcome news to the child-bearing set, that doctors have been able to relieve even difficult cases of nausea and vomiting with vitamins B_1 and B_6 administered intramuscularly or intravenously. In a study done in England of pregnant women suffering with constant vomiting, each patient was given an intramuscular injection of 100 milligrams of thiamine (B_1) every day. As much as 50 percent improvement was noted after the very first injection. After the fourth or fifth injection, the vomiting ceased in every case.

A study reported in the *American Journal of Obstetrics and Gynecology* reveals that complete relief from almost constant nausea and vomiting was achieved by the administration of 25 to 100 milligrams of B_1 and 50 milligrams of B_6. Two of the patients in this study were also relieved of accompanying migraine headaches. None had any undesirable side reactions.

The only difference between getting an injection of a vitamin and eating the vitamin is that the injection puts it into the blood stream immediately. However, if you have been getting enough of these vitamins every day, the chances are you will not reach the point where you cannot hold anything in your stomach and must therefore get it quickly by injection. In fact, if you have been getting plenty of these vitamins, then you have an ample supply in your blood stream at all times and may never experience the nausea of pregnancy.

While nausea has been considered a necessary concomitant of pregnancy, this study reveals that "it ain't necessarily so." There are women whose nutrition is superb who sail through pregnancy without a moment of queasiness.

If large doses of thiamine (B_1) and pyridoxine (B_6) can control this debilitating and depleting condition, then a diet rich in these vitamins will certainly help to prevent it.

Since bananas and yeast are good sources of B_6 and B_1, as well as all the other B's, try this delicious milk shake.

Banana Yeast Shake

2 tablespoons yeast	1 cup certified raw, soy or nut
1 tablespoon soya powder	milk
1 sliced banana	1 teaspoon raw honey
½ teaspoon pure vanilla	½ cup cracked ice
1 cup pure water or unsweetened pineapple juice	

Put water or juice, yeast and soya powder in blender. Whiz. Add milk, ice, honey, vanilla and sliced bananas. Whiz again. Drink in good health.

Other B vitamins shown by various researchers to be of vital importance in preventing some of the usual complications of pregnancy are niacin, choline and folic acid.

Niacin was shown to be particularly effective in preventing toxemia, pre-eclampsia (toxemia of late pregnancy with swelling) and eclampsia (convulsions, edema, and hypertension).

When a pregnant woman suffers with these conditions, she may experience vomiting, high blood pressure, waterlogging of the tissue, convulsions and sometimes coma and death. Obviously these are not conditions to be taken lightly or to be left to chance if there is something you can do to prevent them. You definitely can do something to control your fate.

In some studies obesity and low protein diets were shown to be factors contributing to these conditions. Weight-watching, then, is important for a woman even when she is "eating for two." By increasing her protein intake, cutting down on carbohydrates, and snacking on fruits and vegetables instead of sweets, a pregnant woman can do much to avoid these complications.

The lack of the B vitamin, choline, can contribute to toxemia of pregnancy. Choline is contained in colostrum, the extra-rich fluid with which mothers, by the wisdom of nature, are equipped to provide their new babies in the first days of nursing to give them a good start. Choline has been identified as essential to the health of the heart and blood vessels. It is also needed for healthy livers and kidneys.

Pregnant women, because of the added strain on their kidneys, are subject to kidney ailments and toxemia. A diet rich in choline can help prevent this dangerous complication. Foods especially rich in choline are soybeans, egg yolk, lamb kidney, liver, peas, snap beans, and especially brewer's yeast and wheat germ.

A lack of folic acid in pregnant women leads to megaloblastic anemia of both mother and child. A recent New York City survey, by Dr. A. Leonard Luhby of the New York Medical College, revealed that 22 percent of their 240 pregnant patients were folic acid deficient, and that 35 percent of these women gave birth to deficient infants. Such a deficiency in infants leads to retarded growth and development and to congenital anomalies such as cleft palate, heart defects, and mental retardation. Folic acid deficiency was found to be three times as frequent among the pregnant women with complications.

It is important to bear in mind that folic acid is not included in most prenatal vitamin supplements. It is present, of course, in natural supplements. Liver, wheat germ, brewer's yeast and green leafy vegetables (uncooked) are excellent sources.

The evidence regarding the role of vitamin E in preventing habitual or threatened abortion is also becoming increasingly convincing. Dr. Evan Shute of Canada reported that he could anticipate spontaneous abortion in women with certain types of hormone deficiency and prevent it with vitamin E.

Miscarriage will sometimes occur because the fetus, for some reason, has failed to remain alive. Some of these *in utero* deaths are attributed to an insufficiency of oxygen in the blood supply which the unborn child receives from his mother. Because vitamin E is a prime factor in maintaining a higher oxygen content in the blood, it helps prevent death in the womb.

A mother must have sufficient vitamin K to keep her baby well supplied so that the baby is not subject to hemorrhage (a frequent occurrence due to the thin capillaries in the newborn). When synthetic K is given to the infant to help staunch this bleeding, the baby may develop a serious disease called kernicterus. The unborn child will benefit measurably if vitamin K is given to the mother and will not run the risk of this disease.

High-K foods are spinach, kale, alfalfa, cabbage, cauliflower, green peas, carrot tops, blackstrap molasses, liver, egg yolk, soybean oil and fish liver oil.

Try this Cabbage with Yogurt

4 cups red or green cabbage, shredded	¼ cup apple cider vinegar
1 onion, grated	¼ cup water or stock
3 tablespoons oil	¼ cup yogurt

Sauté cabbage and onion briefly in oil. Add vinegar and stock. Cover and simmer gently for 5 minutes. Remove from heat and blend in yogurt.

Grow some alfalfa sprouts and use them daily in your salads. Soak 3 tablespoons of unsprayed, untreated alfalfa seed in a quart jar. Use plenty of unchlorinated water. Put two layers of cheese cloth over mouth of jar and secure with a rubber band. Next morning drain water from jar through the cheese cloth. Rinse seeds several times. Turn jar upside down and tilt it in a large bowl or on edge of sink so that there is drainage. Gently shake seeds to distribute them around the wall of the jar. Keep in a warm, dark place for two days. After the second day spread seeds thinly on bottom of glass dish. Sprinkle generously with water three times a day. Cover with wet cheesecloth. In about 5 days, your alfalfa sprouts will look like a green carpet. They are now ready for your salads, for beverages or just eating out of hand. They are delicious and a great source of vitamin K.

It would appear that a fresh approach to the problem of obstetrical complication may be found, at least in part, in the field of diet therapy. This is information which should be of tremendous value to every doctor and which no pregnant woman can afford to ignore.

Indeed, in the face of this overwhelming evidence, no expectant mother can sit back and leave her fate to Heaven or to an uninformed obstetrician. The stakes are too high. It is important that every woman should know that she herself, by making good nutrition her first order of business, can in a large measure be the master of her fate and enjoy nine months of glowing expectations crowned with safe harbor for a beautiful, healthy baby.

Chapter VI

It's Safer to Make
Your Own Baby Foods

"Doctor, in view of the recent disclosures about additives in baby foods, should I stop using them?" This question is being posed with increasing frequency as concerned mothers now view with alarm the baby foods they once viewed with such favor.

Pediatricians may or may not advise mothers to discontinue using these baby foods depending on how far ahead they are of government disclosures. After all, a knowledge of what goes into the manufacture of baby foods is not a requisite for graduation from medical school.

Did your pediatrician think to question the safety of monosodium glutamate in baby foods? Dr. John W. Olney of Washington University School of Medicine revealed that MSG produces irreversible eye and brain damage in mice, that it damages the hypothalamus, which controls appetite and thus contributes to obesity, that animals

34

treated with MSG show stunted bone growth and female sterility.

Only because of the widespread publicity given to Dr. Olney's study and the subsequent public indignation did the three major manufacturers of baby foods—Heinz, Gerber, and Beech-Nut—announce in 1969, a moratorium on the use of MSG in their baby foods, pending further tests.

Safety and good nutrition aren't the food industry's strong suits. As disclosed in the testimony of Ralph Nader before the McGovern Senate Investigating Committee, July 15, 1969, "For the domestic food industry there are several important consumer preferences to meet if a particular product is to be commercially successful. These are *taste, texture, tenderness, aesthetics and convenience.* The ingenious misuse of modern chemistry—especially coloring agents, seasonings and preservatives—can meet these preferences. The tragic factor is that these preferences can be met by non-nutritious, contaminated, deteriorating and other adulterated food products. Further, the same chemical tactics that meet these preferences also mask the true condition of the product and dull what sensory detection facilities the consumer has to alert him to wholesome products. The soothing pictures and messages on the packages and in the media further lull the consumer into blind trust."

Baby foods are laced with undesirable additives, other than MSG, which the industry is as yet taking no steps to remove—not because they have been proven safe, but because there has as yet been no public objection to their use.

What about the salt that is causing hypertension, the starch fillers that are displacing the protein you think your baby is getting, the sugar that goes into baby's vegetables, and the nitrates?

If every mother of a precious baby knew what went into those commercial jars of baby food, she would go to any lengths to prepare her own. And, she would find that with a blender and a freezer, making her own would actually take less time than going marketing. It would be far less expensive and the rewards in better health and increased potential for mental growth, as well as physical well-being, would be incalculable.

In the first place, when you make your own baby food, you can eliminate the salt and give your child a far better chance for avoiding hypertension. One scientist, Dr. Lewis

K. Dahl, Medical Research Center, Brookhaven National Laboratory, testified at the hearings of Senator George McGovern's Select Committee on Nutrition and Human Needs that processed baby-food meats contain five to six times the amount of salt in unprocessed meat, processed vegetables have six to 60 times the natural amount, and dry cereals 100 times as much. He pointed out, too, that infants and children can get all the salt they need from natural foods.

Salt is added to practically all baby foods, simply to appeal to the mother's taste—not the baby's. He'd probably like it much better without the salt. Salt has caused high blood pressure in laboratory rats and conceivably could have the same effect in babies.

And how did Dr. Dahl induce the hypertensive states in these animals? By feeding them the same foods you are giving the baby. He fed them solely with mixtures of commercially available baby foods. After only 4 months, 5 of the 7 test rats had developed hypertension. But the 7 control animals, who were also hypertension-prone but were fed on low-salt food, enjoyed normal blood pressure levels.

Dr. Dahl told the committee that he believes these data are relevant to man, and, until proved otherwise, they have been interpreted to mean that "the younger the organism, the greater will be the susceptibility to developing hypertension from salt; as the amount and duration of salt consumption increase, the probability of hypertension will increase; and among those with a genetic predisposition to hypertension, (whose parents or grandparents suffered with high blood pressure, for instance) *even transient high salt intakes may induce permanent hypertension.*" (emphasis ours)

In other words, the earlier you start your baby on commercial baby foods, the greater his chances of suffering hypertension either now or later in life.

"One of the enduring characteristics of the food industry," Nader pointed out, "is its penchant to sell now and have someone else test later. In case after case, the sequence of doubt to risk to reasonable certainty of harm has been the burden of researchers outside the food industry. It comes as a highly disturbing disclosure that this sequence is emerging for the one area of food product in which most people hold greatest trust. I am speaking of baby food."

The mother who blends her own baby food can lessen her baby's chances of suffering respiratory failure now, and sterility later, by preparing meats and vegetables without nitrite or nitrates. Nitrates are added to meats to keep the products colored red or to make them look fresher than they are. Sodium nitrate gives baby foods longer shelf life and preserves the pink color in cured meats. But nitrates reduce the blood's ability to carry oxygen. Thus, in sufficient quantity, they can lead to respiratory failure, even death.

Dr. Barry Commoner, Director of the Center for the Biology of the Natural Systems, Washington University, St. Louis, Missouri, told the American Association for the Advancement of Science that certain commercial baby foods—beets and spinach—contained as much as 0.8 percent nitrate.

Another additive that usually isn't reckoned with is modified starch used as a filler. Some babies are allergic, not to the food their mothers are giving them intentionally, but, to the cornstarch or tapioca which has been surreptitiously added to it. Even if the baby is not allergic, the use of starch in baby foods cheats the baby of the food values he needs. Meat is given to babies because it contains blood-building iron, copper, amino acids, and other nutritional necessities. But in certain processed foods, some of the meat is replaced by starch.

When you feed your baby meat, you want him to have the full protein value of that meat—undiluted. Some infants have a very small capacity for food and to fill up that small space with an empty starch when what he needs is protein is cheating him of his full potential for growth.

True, when baby foods were first marketed they spelled a sort of emancipation for the busy mother. Today, with a blender and a freezer, making baby's food is no more of a chore than making your food, and it gives you an opportunity to enrich your baby's food with highly nutritive ingredients like wheat germ and yeast.

Judith R. Hinds, a mother who makes her own, calls it *Dab* Cookery. With a minimum of planning, baby meals in the form of dabs can be made in advance and frozen.

To make dabs, you steam or simmer fruits and vegetables, preferably organically grown, just as you would for your family, using very little water and being careful not to overcook. Puree the foods in the blender using all of the cooking liquid which is rich in minerals. If the mixture is runny, add wheat germ. Meats can be steamed or lightly sautéed and then finely chopped. Or you can make a meat and vegetable combination in the blender. The vegetable juice will provide sufficient liquid for proper blending.

Once the puree is ready, simply drop the mixture, like pancake batter, by the tablespoon onto a plate. The size of the dab is determined by your baby's appetite. For his first foods, a teaspoonful may be enough. As he grows, increase the amount and blend for a shorter time. This will encourage chewing. Next, put the plate in the freezer for several hours. When the dabs are frozen solid, store them in a covered container.

Mrs. Hinds suggests that when you are ready to use the dabs, simply thaw them in a covered pyrex dish for several hours in the refrigerator, then heat on a warming tray or a yogurt maker or simply over warm water in a double boiler. Presto! Baby can have pure unadulterated food with no more trouble than going to the store to stock up—maybe even less. You can even take dabs along on trips; simply keep them cold in the car cooler.

Here are some of Mrs. Hinds' recipes. You can adapt the same procedure to other food such as apples, prunes, pears, squash, sweet potatoes, eggplant, anything you grow in your garden, and to such meat as beef heart, calf's brain, liver or fish.

For iron-rich apricot dabs, simmer one or two pounds of sun-dried unsulphured apricots for 30 minutes in pure water to cover. Let stand until cool. Blend the apricots with the liquid until smooth, then make and freeze dabs as described. You can double the number of dabs, give them a nice flavor, and increase the nutrients by stirring into the puree half again as much yogurt. Baby will love the creamy consistency and the yogurt will help him develop a good healthy intestinal flora.

To make chicken liver dabs, Mrs. Hinds suggests that you steam 2 carrots along with 4 stalks of chopped celery and one small onion until tender (for about ten minutes). Place in blender with liquid. Now sauté one pound of chicken livers lightly, or steam them until they change color. Chop coarsely. Now blend with vegetables by flicking switch on and off at the start. This will make quite a few dabs. Mrs. Hinds leaves ¾ of the mixture in the blender, adds nuts, hard-cooked eggs, one chopped onion and curry powder for a delicious dish for the whole family.

Another way to feed your baby healthfully is to give him the same nutritious food you give to the rest of your family. Chicken soup with brown rice? Baby will love it. Hamburger? Let him crumble his own. If you're having stew, put some chunks of meat and vegetables through the blender. Are you having steak or lamb chops? That high chair thumper will have a ball with a meaty bone. The same vegetables you're serving to the family can be pureed for a few seconds in the blender and given to baby.

While the family is eating salad, baby can go to town on a piece of celery or a carrot stick. He can join you for a mashed baked potato right out of the jacket. For dessert, try fresh fruit. Baby's share can be pureed in the blender. It's far superior to the fruit that is processed, sweetened and sold in jars.

If you have a source of organically grown apples, pears, or apricots, cook up a batch with their mineral rich skins. Use no sugar. Use a little raw honey as your only sweetener. Freeze. Defrost on a winter's day and serve it chunky to the family and pureed for baby.

Use your own ingenuity. Go creative. Why relegate the sacred task of providing your baby's food to some impersonal manufacturer whose first consideration is profit?

If your pediatrician tells you that baby foods in the jars are the purest foods you can possibly get, he hasn't been doing his homework. Unfortunately, many new mothers have so little confidence in their own maternal wisdom that they won't make a move until they get their pediatrician's explicit approval. When I suggested to a new mother that she might give her baby a fertile egg right out of its own shell and an ungassed banana right from its natural protective peel instead of macerated egg yolk and mashed banana that's been processed and stuffed into a baby food jar, she said, "Oh really? I'll have to ask my pediatrician about that."

Use your good old common sense and your inborn maternal wisdom; give your baby tender loving care and nutritious foods you have prepared yourself. I know of no greater source of satisfaction and no better investment in your baby's future.

Chapter VII

Lollipops—
Reward or Punishment?

The mother who says, "Don't cry, honey, here's a cookie," the doting grandparents who express love with lollipops and chocolate brownies are perhaps the worst enemies of the children they love so very much.

Not only are these sweet treats leading to cavities, a sweet tooth, and hypoglycemia, they are also starting the children on the road to obesity. And a fat child has two strikes against him before he even gets to the ball field.

A fat child is often an unhappy child who misses out on much of the fun and games. Unless a serious effort is made to normalize his weight, he tends to become a fat teenager and a fat adult, forever fighting the battle of the bulge, forever trying fad diets to the detriment of his health, suffering all the health complications that go with overweight—high blood pressure, liver and gall bladder disease urinary tract diseases, hernias and diabetes or hypoglycemia

Unfortunately, many parents tend to view their child's extra blubber without too much concern. "He'll grow out of it,' they say. But studies of fat children who have grown up, but not out of their excess poundage, belie this kind of casual approach to the problem. Most of them *don't* grow out of it. They grow heavier.

It is the nature of obesity that it tends to perpetuate itself—it slows down metabolism so that even restricted calories seem to go to fat; it slows down movement so that the heavy child does not burn up calories at the rate that Johnnie, who is forever playing stick ball, does, and it discourages participation in the kind of group activity which is so essential to the morale of the child.

Leading medical authorities are finding that just being fat is a serious threat to our children both physically and emotionally and they are genuinely alarmed at the enormous numbers of overweight children in our population.

From coast to coast, statistics show that already more than ten-million young people up to nineteen are burdened with excess poundage. The problem is a serious one now and threatens to become more serious.

It goes without saying that the best way to beat the problem of obesity is to prevent it in the first place. What makes a child fat? According to psychiatrist Dr. Hilda Bruch, the problem may well start in the perambulator. (*The Importance of Overweight*, Norton, New York, 1957.) She points up an interesting relationship, between food and a baby's emotions, which every mother should ponder. Many times a baby will cry because he wants some cuddling and comfort, or a change of scene. But, Dr. Bruch points out, a mother frequently thrusts a bottle in the mouth of her crying infant instead of holding him. It is only natural that the child should link the satisfaction of eating with his emotional needs. The link between food and emotional satisfaction persists as the child grows up.

Another avenue by which children travel the road to obesity is paved with a mother's over-zealous competitive spirit. It's time young mothers stopped considering their infant's ability to guzzle new foods as their own personal merit badge.

If you tune in on the conversation of a group of mothers tending their perambulators at the park or by the front stoop, you'll hear conversational snatches that attest to this spirit. "Can you imagine, he ate a whole jar of mixed lamb and vegetables—and he's only three months old." "My Johnnie is only six weeks old and already loves his pablum."

The mother whose baby is getting no more than formula is envious. She's going to pester her pediatrician until he prescribes some solid food for her baby, too.

And it's not just the mother—the baby's doctor, too, is largely responsible, Dr. M. J. Oldfield of Thirsk, Yorkshire, chides the pediatrician in the correspondence section of *The British Medical Journal* (October 5, 1968). "On every side we hear of the problem of the fat child who grows into the obese adult with all the well-known attendant hazards," he writes.

"As a general practitioner, I am, therefore, more than a little dismayed to hear of the rather disastrous advice given to my young mothers by visiting and clinic public health personnel, this advice being to start supplementary fat-making carbohydrate feeding from the early age of 3 or 4 weeks, whether the baby be breast-or-bottle-fed, not only giving the new and often apprehensive mother unnecessary added work, anxiety, and expense, but also laying down an unhealthy feeding pattern for life. Can it be that commercial pressures are so strong that they can stuff the public health authorities, who in turn persuade the mothers to stuff their children in the erroneous belief that nature is absentmindedly allowing birth to take place unaccompanied by the provision of a prefabricated, prepacked, precooked cereal?"

Because recent statistics unfold so somber a picture of overweight as a cradle-to-early-grave phenomenon, doctors are now taking a concerned look at the adorably dimpled one-year-old whose arms and legs are creased with fat. The fact is, that while many babies slim down in the toddler years, a significant number do not. One half of all fat children are seriously overweight by their sixth birthday. Yet, mothers do not realize the gravity of the problem and sometimes wait for years before seeking help. When one doctor weighed in a 12-year-old at 200 pounds, he threw up his hands and wailed, "Why didn't her mother do something 80 pounds ago?"

Fat children suffer exclusion from their group and suffer psychological traumas as a result. In a study in depth conducted by L. Monello and Dr. Jean Mayer of Harvard, it was found that personality traits among obese adolescents were strikingly similar to the traits sociologists have shown to be typical of youngsters in oppressed minority groups who were victims of intense prejudice.

Dr. Frederick Werkman and Elsa S. Greenberg, Ph.D., of George Washington University School of Medicine and the Division of Adolescent Psychiatry at the Children's Hospital in Washington, D.C., conducted a study at a medically oriented summer camp for overweight girls and found a great deal of psychic discomfort and depression. "An obese girl," they said, "misses many adolescent experiences; she loses independence and a chance to learn more about life. She avoids challenges and tends to settle for the humdrum. This affects the future course of her life."

At what age is obesity a problem? That which develops before the age of 10 or after the age of 16 is the kind which persists and presents a continual problem. That which develops just before the onset of puberty may be an exaggeration of a normal physiologic process and is often self-correcting in the next few years, says Dr. Jean Mayer.

This kind of weight gain should not be treated as a problem lest it become a problem, Dr. Mayer advises. It is probably not only useless but perhaps dangerous to treat this transient increase in weight as though it were obesity to be corrected at once, Dr. Mayer warns. First, underfeeding a child just before his main growth spurt may jeopardize the increase in height, which of itself would eliminate the abnormality in height-weight ratio. In addition, calling the child's attention to this temporary unsightliness may give him an image of himself as "fat and ugly" and cause him to withdraw from activities with his peers, thus causing more weight gain and considerable unhappiness. This leads to the habit of seeking solace from food, more withdrawal from society, more inactivity and obesity that clouds his life right up to and through adulthood.

It isn't only what he eats, but what he does or does not do that can make a child fat. If he continues to eat heartily but discontinues the running and jumping and climbing that was second nature to his lean years, he's going to get fat. This was dramatically demonstrated by experiments on animals and in adult men conducted by Dr. Mayer. Actually, Mayer found, when activity was low, food intake, both in experimental animals and in men, tended to increase. This is a phenomenon long known to farmers who coop up or pen their animals in order to fatten them.

Inactivity can contribute to weight gain and obesity certainly contributes to inactivity. Here is a powerful argument for parents to introduce the joy of physical activity, participation in active sports, nature walks, swimming when their children are very young, especially if they show a tendency to be sedentary. Because, once they get fat, it's very hard to get them moving.

Granted, that much of this advice might help to prevent your slim child from becoming overweight. But what about the child who is already a fatty? What's a mother to do?

There is much that a mother can do but first let me stress what she should not do. She should never coax, cajole, nag, threaten or bribe. Never shame your child or use derogatory nicknames like fatty, porky, tubby. She should never insist piously on a display of will power.

What can a mother do? She can have ready for him a highly nutritious, low calorie snack when he comes home from school ravenous—some cold sliced meat or freshly broiled chicken livers, grated carrots mixed with raisins or some Waldorf salad—chopped apples, celery and walnuts tossed with a little mayonnaise or yogurt, served with a tall glass of vegetable juice. This kind of attention says "lovin' " much more meaningfully than a chocolate cake in the oven.

Bear in mind that nine out of ten of the nation's overweight are suffering with hypoglycemia. Since an overweight child, according to the studies, is more than likely traveling the road to hypoglycemia, it would be a wise parent who anticipated this eventuality and sought to prevent the condition by adhering to the principles of the hypoglycemic diet, which is one which will promote both weight loss and good health. It is one which the whole family will benefit by, whether they are fatties or twiggies, because the sound nutrition principles on which it is based tend to normalize the weight.

This diet is based on high protein (lean meat, eggs, fish), moderate fat (predominately of the polyunsaturated type) and low carbohydrates. Use absolutely no empty calories—no white sugar nor white flour products. Avoid overprocessed foods. Stress fruits and vegetables *in the raw*—preferably organically grown so that they have their full complement of vitamins, minerals and enzymes. Avoid the foods that are high in calories and low in nutrients—potato chips, popcorn, candy, pastry, soft drinks. Go easy on the salt shaker—use herb seasonings as much as possible. If your family is accustomed to desserts, wean them away from cakes and pies. Serve instead wedges of apples, pears, oranges or melon—any fruit in season is a fine finale for a meal and it leaves a fresh clean taste.

If you really want to help your child lose weight, says Gussie Mason in her book, *How to Help Your Child Lose Weight* (Hawthorn Books, New York, 1969), start with his breakfast. If you let your child get his own breakfast, she warns, you can forget your hopes for his diet. "Chances are he won't have time or go to the trouble to eat what he needs to sustain him until lunch." This triggers the mid-morning candy bar syndrome that plays havoc with one's waistline.

A concerned mother will rise early and start her child's dieting day in the right way, says Mrs. Mason, who runs two camps for overweight children. "When you can't get him out of bed until the last minute, prepare an eggnog— 2 eggs, one glass skim milk, one teaspoon vanilla and a dash of nutmeg." I say soy or nut milk, instead of skim milk.

On weekends you can put more thought and time into breakfast. Try scrambling eggs with mushrooms, green pepper or onion; add chopped pimientos or bean sprouts; make omelets with stewed tomatoes. Such a breakfast will make the whole family happy.

A wise mother, up on the facts of good nutrition, can make some wise substitutions in her family's diet. She can deftly eliminate all the empty calories, the overprocessed foods, the noodles, macaroni, white rice, all the sugared concoctions; serve instead an increasing variety of vegetables, grow her own sprouts for added salad interest and for added vitamins, minerals and enzymes.

Try this for raves. It's chock full of nutrients, good flavor and contains scarcely any calories.

Red Cabbage and Mung Bean Sprouts Sauté

3 tablespoons safflower oil	1 tablespoon caraway seeds
4 cups shredded red cabbage	sea salt and paprika to taste
2 cups mung bean sprouts	

In a large, heavy skillet, heat the oil and sauté cabbage and sprouts for about 5 minutes or until tender-crisp. Add caraway seeds and seasonings and toss lightly. Serve hot.

Instead of french fries, try broiled onion.

Broiled Onions

Has all the goodness of the onion without frying.
Slice large onions ½ inch thick. Make a dip of vegetable oil

and herb seasonings. Coat the onion well with this dip. Broil on both sides till lightly browned.

She should little by little introduce organ meats—they are lower in calories and higher in nutrition than the more expensive muscle meats. Liver, heart, lung, brain can be served in many enticing ways.

Try this recipe for Beef Heart Chow.

Beef Heart Chow

1 pound beef heart	1½ cups stewed tomatoes
2 tablespoons soy flour	½ cup diced green pepper
3 tablespoons oil	dash of paprika
1 onion, finely diced	¾ cup brown rice
1 clove garlic, crushed	1 tablespoon nutritional yeast
1 cup tomato sauce	

Cut heart into one-inch cubes, dredge with flour. Sauté in hot oil, 5 to 10 minutes. Remove. Sauté onion, pepper, and garlic in same oil. Return heart. Add rest of ingredients except yeast. Cover and simmer 35 minutes, adding hot water if necessary to prevent sticking Do not stir. Shake the pan once or twice. Add yeast. Rice should be tender.

There is much that a mother can do in the kitchen that will help her unhappy fat child lose weight. True, it will take more time and thought, but the rewards are definitely worth the effort. (She'll find her own figure improving, too.)

A Simple, Healthful Reducing Plan

Breakfast: 1 large glass of fresh, raw fruit or vegetable juice
1 cup fresh berries or other fresh fruit
1 average portion (about 4 oz.) of broiled liver or fresh fish—or 2 eggs, boiled
1 cup herb tea or a glass of soybean milk

Lunch: For the light meal of the day, you can try your own variation of this menu:
1 cup fresh fruit
1 serving of lean meat, such as chicken or broiled, lean hamburger—or a fresh vegetable plate of, say, sliced tomatoes, cucumbers, carrots, and asparagus
1 serving of homemade applesauce (no sugar)
1 glass of fresh juice

Supper: For the large meal of the day, how about something like this:
A relish tray of iced fresh vegetables (whole small

tomatoes, celery stalks, green peppers, etc.)

1 serving of lean meat (baked or broiled, such as steak, veal, or lamb chops, liver, turkey, etc.)

1 medium-sized serving of brown rice

1 hot, fresh vegetable, simply prepared, such as spinach, broccoli, cauliflower, string beans, etc. (Emphasize the green and yellow ones.)

A large salad bowl, brimming with as many varieties of lettuce as you can find, tossed in a salad oil, (sunflower, soy or corn oil), sprinkled with freshly-chopped herbs such as oregano, parsley, mint, chives, etc. (You need a fresh salad daily for the unsaturated fatty acids in the oil you use for a dressing, as well as the nutrients you get from raw vegetables.)

Fresh pineapple wedges for dessert

1 cup herb tea

Chapter VIII

Teens Need More Nutrition and Are Getting Less

If your teenager is an under-achiever, given to emotional outbursts, nervous, tired, impossible, welcome to the club. And take heart. In all probability there is no need to rush him to a psychiatrist. As a far more practical measure you can take yourself, *check his nutrition*.

Even though he seems to be forever eating, studies indicate that the teenager is actually the poorest fed member of the American family. In fact, if your teenager is going along with the crowd and consuming the usual teenage diet, he is not only undermining his mental stability but is setting the stage for later problems, including heart disease, kidney disease, allergies, overweight, emotional disturbances and heartbreaking complications with his own children.

48

A report from Rutgers University College of Agriculture and Environmental Science (August, 1967) disclosed that as many as six out of every ten teenage girls and four out of every ten teenage boys have poor diets.

At the same time, girls are marrying earlier and having children earlier, says Dr. Evelyn Spindler, nutritionist of the U.S. Department of Agriculture. "Many American teenage girls are so undernourished that as young mothers they put in peril their ability to bear children," Dr. Spindler warned. "In addition, some birth defects and some deaths at time of delivery can be traced directly to the undernourishment of the mother. Their babies may be born prematurely, have congenital defects or inadequate nutritional stores to see them through the birth process."

Why are teenagers so poorly fed? On the whole, many surveys reveal, they tend to skip breakfast because they are rushed and no one prepares it for them. Many eat no citrus fruit. Some will skip lunch, too, because they are trying to achieve a glamorous figure. Many subsist on snacks, candy bars and Cokes. One of the contributing factors to the inadequate teenage diet is the poor selection of food for snacks, Dr. Spindler points out. They are often "empty calorie foods made chiefly of fat, sugar and starches with vitamins and minerals woefully lacking."

Studies show that omission of breakfast decreases the work rate and is detrimental to attitudes and scholastic performance. Research disclosed that girls who missed fewer meals than other girls scored best in emotional stability, conformity, adjustment to reality and family relationships. Generally, adolescents who have more information about nutritional needs have better diets.

Another popular practice, which contributes to poor nutrition in boys, is the practice of encouraging them to adopt drastic reducing diets for lower weight classifications in boxing or wrestling. Boys who must lose anywhere from 5 to 25 pounds in a few weeks, at a time in their lives when they should normally be gaining weight steadily, often dehydrate their bodies with steam baths, epsom salt baths and low fluid intake. They sometimes starve on diets of 400 to 500 calories daily.

Here we have the compelling motive of victory on the playing field mitigating against good health. While medical authorities condemn this practice, it is quite common, not only on the college level, but in junior highs and high schools. Here, indeed, is a practice which parents and P.T.A. groups should investigate.

The Rutgers report cited earlier revealed that the nutrients most often lacking in teenage diets are *iron* (especially low in the diets of teenage girls), *vitamin C, vitamin A, thiamine, riboflavin* and *calcium.*

Contrary to their public image, teenagers are not full of boundless vim, vigor and exuberant good health. According to a nationwide survey conducted by the Purdue University Opinion Panel, teenagers are worried about their health and feel that they tire too easily. Almost half of the thousands of young people interviewed complained of having no pep, and more than a third were bothered by upset stomachs, eye difficulties, frequent headaches and colds. One-fourth said they had no appetite and one out of five thought his hearing was defective.

Dr. Pauline Beery Mack, well known nutrition authority, came to the alarming conclusion that American teenagers, even those of high-income families, are gravely undernourished. Her ten-year study of some 2,500 boys and girls between the ages of 13 and 20 years was conducted under the sponsorship of the Pennsylvania State Department of Health.

Here, indeed, is a clear mandate for parents and school administrators, who must not abdicate their responsibility for what their teenagers eat.

There is much that can be done by school administrators and by parents to make good eating habits the "In" thing.

Mrs. Gena Larson, cafeteria manager at Helix High School in San Diego County, instituted a *school lunch program* that proved what good nutrition can do, not only in the improvement of athletic skills, but also in terms of academic achievements and in the improvement of reading habits and resolving personality problems.

Her approach was to crack down on the sugar foods. For dessert, students were given a choice of a frozen orange juice bar, gelatin or fresh fruit. Supplements were used liberally in the preparation of the food including wheat germ, bone meal, soy flour and rice polish. Good food values were contained in other regulars, including raw carrots, celery, apple, boysenberry and orange juices. Snacks included raisins, sunflower seeds, pumpkin seeds and wheat germ flakes.

The California Youth Authority applauded the improved nutrition at Helix High as bringing about improved dental health (fewer cavities), better emotional health, better citizenship and better grades. In fact, "The CYA thinks we may have one of the answers to the dropout problem,"

Mrs. Larson said. "They feel there is a relationship between nutritional habits and delinquency."

Mrs. Larson admitted that occasionally there were gripes about the lack of white bread, substitution of carob powder for chocolate, raw honey and ground dates for sugar. "We can't really taste the difference," said a football player and student body president, "but it just gives us something to beef about." And every parent knows that if a teener doesn't have something to beef about, he'll beef about not having anything to beef about.

While the school can and should contribute in a large measure to the nutrition of our teenagers, much of the stimulus for good eating habits must come from the home. Here the responsibility rests with mother, you, the kitchen wizard, who has it within her power to shape the destiny of her loved ones.

"No longer can mothers blithely send their children off to school after serving them a bowl of their favorite cereal, confident that they are full of nutritious body-building food." That's what Senator Frank Moss said after hearing charges that 40 of the leading dry breakfast cereals were so low in nutritional content that they constituted "empty calories" (*New York Times*, July 23, 1970).

"I urge American consumers to take heed," Senator Moss warned. "The 'Breakfast of Champions' or Tony the Tiger's favorite cereal may be letting us down."

This blast against the nutritionless "empty calorie," foodless cereals that fill almost two aisles in every supermarket and are ballyhooed with circus-like fanfare as the answer to every child's dream of glory in the playground, on the ballfield and in the ballroom, came as a real shocker to the cereal-eating public.

The charge against the cereals, with brands identified, was made before a Senate consumer subcommittee by Robert B. Choate, Jr., a citizen lobbyist on the issue of hunger. It was Choate who helped to stimulate national interest in hunger, a subject which previously was largely discounted as not relevant to the United States—"the land of plenty."

Choate charged, too, that the worst cereals are huckstered to children watching Saturday morning TV.

It is true that the cereal industry in their advertising and promotions concentrate their best creative efforts on catching the mother through her child who sets up a loud squawk at the market unless he can have the breakfast of chumps or the snap, crackle and flop kind.

Trade sources estimate that there is some $80 million

worth of dry cereal advertising over a year, most of it in television and about 30 percent to 40 percent of the ad dollars directed at the kiddies.

Mr. Choate aimed another blast at Federal agencies. They do not protect the public, he emphasized. "They have been more worried about the economics of the market place than about meeting the nutritional needs of the budget-dominated American family."

In his recent testimony, Mr. Choate further blasted the cereal manufacturers because, in their advertising, they were "counter-educating children away from nutrition knowledge." He said that children were being misled by heroic television advertising, by gifts and prizes and *by a reliance on sugar flavorings.*

The addition of sugar (to cereals) is now very common and dietetically most objectionable. Indeed, many of today's so called breakfast foods contain more sugar than they do wheat or corn, and become confections, rather than good wholesome food.

The consumer will do well not to purchase breakfast cereals in which sugar is either first or second on the list of ingredients. (Ingredients named on packaged foods are named in order of their predominance by weight in the mixture, so that substances present in the largest amounts appear at the beginning of the list of ingredients.)

Actually, Mr. Choate was too kind. He blasted the cereal industry only for the lack of nutrients in their highly-touted products. He might have added a further well-deserved blast for the use of BHT and BHA in their products as "freshness preservers." If you have taken the trouble to read the fine print on the cereal boxes lately, you will note that there are precious few that do not include these chemicals. These cereals, then, can be not only a poor food nutritionally, they can contribute to a dangerous build-up of chemicals in your body.

Dr. Michael Latham, professor of international nutrition at Cornell University, recommended "an investigation, and hopefully a restriction, of subtle, often false insinuations made by breakfast-cereal advertisers which lead the public to believe that these foods have nutritional qualities which are superior to many cheaper, and often more nutritious, ordinary foods such as bread."

If you start the children when they are young on good hearty breakfasts, rich in protein, tasty-but-healthful lunches and dinners, good substantial snack food and juices, in place of sodas, they will not depart from these habits when they become teenagers and adults. The rewards in radiant health, achievement and personal fulfillment cannot be calculated.

The parent who helps youngsters to understand nutrition needs, who helps the teenager to realize that he is "with it" and "doing his own thing" when he shuns empty calories and eats useful food, will do a great service to young people —and may have an extra bonus in the discovery of ways to improve his own food habits.

Chapter IX

How to Take the Blue Out of Monday

How is your disposition today? Do you feel cheerful, confident and capable of coping with the children no matter what mischief they contrive? How about the children? Are they cheerful, confident and rarin' to go? Or are they mopey, dopey and fearful of their teachers, their recitations and their competence?

If you are like the majority of Americans, you don't feel able to cope at all. In fact, you feel rotten and depressed much of the time, and for no apparent reason. Every job seems too much to tackle. The children get on your nerves. You are unable to make decisions. You've got the blues. Depression with its sidekicks, lethargy and lack of energy, is one of the most prevalent chronic diseases in the world.

But, take heart. There's much magic you can conjure up in your kitchen that will make you and your family different from the crowd in many delightful ways. You can manipulate the menu to make sure all the elements that nourish the psyche as well as the soma are bountiful in your meals and snacks. For example, blood sugar levels that yo-yo from high to low frequently cause emotional problems, and much physical distress, too. You can serve the kind of foods that keep blood sugar on an even keel.

Before we go into menus and recipes that will help overcome the blue Mondays that stretch into every day of the week, let's take a look at the food elements that have a particular relevance to morale and to mental health. Why don't we get them in the course of eating a so-called normal balanced diet?

Maybe you don't know that if your system is deprived of even a single food chemical, your mental state might suffer. That if you go on a cockeyed reducing diet you are bound to deprive your body of important elements. Perhaps it is not just an accident of genes that some people are perpetual sourpusses while others exude good humor and optimism—even people of the same family, eating at the same table. We all know that one child will help himself to doubles on mashed potatoes while another will double on the salad—one will reach for an apple, another for a doughnut or a candy bar.

How can you be sure that no one in your family, however erratic his eating habits may be, is not being deprived of some essential food element? This is a real challenge to today's sneaky cook. "Eat a balanced diet and you'll get all the food elements you need," may have been true before our grains were refined, processed and adulterated with additives. It is not true today. And that is one big reason why so many of us, including doctors, are leading tired listless lives and living through blue Mondays every day in the week.

Let's consider the role pantothenic acid (also called calcium pantothenate) plays in the way you feel. This is one of the vitamins left on the milling room floor in the flour refining process. Those lacking in it may suffer the vague pains of neuritis, lack of energy, an inability to think clearly and lapses of memory. Serious deficiencies lead to alarming symptoms of apathy, depression, heart abnormalities, abdominal pains, susceptibility to infections, impairment of the adrenal glands and disorders of the nerves and muscles which have been corrected when the vitamin was supplied. Pantothenic acid has an antihistamine effect, which acts favorably against allergies. Pantothenic acid is important to the body's use of fats and carbohydrates. It supports certain intestinal bacteria thought to synthesize B vitamins. Indirectly then a shortage of pantothenic acid could cause a lack of other B vitamins.

To keep your good physical health and a cheerful disposition, you should get between five and ten milligrams of pantothenic acid daily. But where? In the *wheat germ removed* from the flour that goes into bread, doughnuts, cookies, cake, macaroni and spaghetti products. Another very good source is liver (about 5 milligrams in one-quarter of a pound or an average serving). Other good meat sources of pantothenic acid are kidneys, heart, spleen, brain, pancreas (sweetbreads), tongue and lungs. Muscle meats (steaks and roasts) are lowest. Frying does not destroy the pantothenic acid in liver; cooking actually seems to improve it! But stewing does cut its potency in kidneys, heart, and spleen by one-third.

Look for pantothenic acid in many of the same foods that contain the other B vitamins—yeast, egg yolk, peanuts, rice bran, broccoli, salmon, soybeans.

There must be something on tonight's dinner menu that you can enrich with a good source of pantothenic acid. Are you making soup? Add two heaping tablespoons of powdered or flaked yeast just before you serve it. It will enhance the flavor and help to improve everyone's disposition.

Another nutrient that can help put smiles on the faces of your loved ones is niacin (vitamin B_3).

We have known for many years that complete lack of niacin causes pellagra, a disease characterized by a severe depression, reminiscent of the schizophrenic patient. Dr. Abraham Hoffer, eminent psychiatrist and director of psychiatric research for Saskatchewan's Department of Public Health, uses massive doses of niacin in treating schizophrenia. With it he has been able to rescue many, many patients from the "snake pit" of so-called "incurables." Dr. Hoffer is convinced that we could eliminate schizophrenia and sharply reduce all other mental illnesses merely by placing sufficient amounts of nicotinamide or niacin in cereal products, enough to give each person at least one gram a day. "This idea," Dr. Hoffer concedes, "would be considered so crazy by most psychiatrists, that I do not expect to see it tested out in my lifetime."

Some day, I have no doubt, the value of niacin in the prevention of schizophrenia will be no less acceptable than vitamin C for preventing scurvy, vitamin B_1 against beriberi and vitamin A as a weapon against night blindness. Scientists concede that there is a lag of some 30 years between the test tube and the dinner table. Why wait to enjoy the benefits of B_3? Dr. Hoffer has shown that there are no dangers connected with its use (it is far safer than aspirin). So he uses it to lower high cholesterol and fat levels in the blood, as well as for schizophrenia and other mental ills.

Malnutrition is no respecter of bankbooks, especially for those persons who have little knowledge of what happens to the foods which are supposed to be providing a "balanced" diet.

The house physician at our local hospital, who performs the histories and physicals on new patients, tells me that she is amazed at the number of patients who show signs of vitamin deficiencies—especially the patients in the psychiatric ward. "But," she says, "it is almost impossible to convince the patient's doctor that this is the case. Mrs. Maslow, deficient in vitamin B? Impossible! She's a rich woman."

Do you begin to see the parts of the puzzle fitting together? Any nutrient relieves the symptoms caused by its lack. If niacin can help to cure schizophrenia, it should be just as effective in preventing it. And, if a severe niacin shortage can cause schizophrenia, might a mild deficiency cause blue Mondays, depression, gloom?

Symptoms of niacin deficiency are everywhere. Look around you. You will probably notice that many friends and neighbors, not just the members of your own family, suffer from one or another of these warning signs: tender gums, diarrhea, nausea, insomnia, indigestion, abdominal pain, irritability, loss of appetite, neurasthenia, anxiety, dizziness, fatigue, numbness in various parts of the body, backache, headache, melancholy, depression. Even a cheerful, pleasant, optimistic person may become tired, apprehensive, and pessimistic, when the body's need for niacin is not being met.

Niacin is another one of the B vitamins which lands on the milling room floor in the refining process. The so-called enrichment program restores one-third of the original amount—and that is a synthetic form which the body does not utilize well. Isn't it ridiculous to remove the real thing in the first place? Some day the refining of grains will be outlawed. But I'm not going to wait. This food element is so important, I don't want to shortchange my family on it.

So where do you get niacin? One of the best sources is yeast. I'm talking about brewer's yeast—not baking yeast. There's a big difference. Uncooked baker's yeast contains live yeast plant cells, great for raising bread, but a threat to unassimilated B complex vitamins in your body. The yeast plants are killed by the heat during the baking process and, once dead, can no longer play havoc with your digestive tract.

Brewer's yeast, sometimes called nutritional yeast, is on the other hand, a rich storehouse of human nutrition, the best natural source of minerals, enzymes, and protein, and all the B vitamins, those known and those yet to be identified. It contains practically no fat, starch or sugar.

Because it is an excellent protein, brewer's yeast sticks to the ribs, satisfies the appetite, improves metabolism and provides the vigor to tackle jobs you've been pushing aside—like cleaning out closets or writing a book. It's a great reducing food, helps to keep blood sugar levels on an even keel and, because it is an excellent source of niacin and thiamine vitamin B_1 (another nerve-saver), it helps to prevent those week-long blue Mondays.

Now, how do you get brewer's yeast into your family? Don't tell my kids, but I add it to everything—soups, stews, baked goods, hamburger mixtures—you name it. I find it gives a wholesome body-warming quality that is most pleasant and, in some subtle way, it does enhance flavors.

If you're subject to the blues, here's a tip for you. Take a yeast break instead of a coffee break. Add a heaping tablespoon of brewer's yeast to a cup of hot water, spike it with a good herb seasoner and presto! You've got a heart-warming pick-up that will chase your cares away.

Another vitamin to help you and your family find the silver lining behind every cloud is thiamine (B_1), sometimes called the "morale" vitamin because, without it, your nerves tend to fray.

Thiamine is so important to your brain that even a mild deficiency for as long as a month is risky. The earliest symptoms of thiamine deficiency are so commonplace that they are frequently ignored. The person lacking in vitamin B_1 lacks energy and is constantly tired. He neither eats well nor sleeps well, and he tends to be cross and irritable.

If your sweet, lovable baby has been "impossible" lately, given to crying spells for no reason at all, look to his thiamine intake just as a safety precaution.

Much of the irritability in people who give you a hard

time at the shopping centers or on the highway could be traced to a B$_1$ deficiency. "Dietary studies, where records are made of the kind and amounts of foods eaten by individuals or families, and then the nutrient content of the diets calculated, indicate that many groups do not receive adequate amounts of thiamine," says Miriam E. Lowenberg in *Food and Man* (John Wiley and Sons, Inc., 1968). "Often dietary lack of thiamine is not so great as to cause definite illness, but the intake is not enough for good health," Dr. Lowenberg says.

Even when there is no definite illness but you're just not feeling "up to par" there may be changes going on in your brain—some of them irreversible. Memory becomes faulty, concentration span becomes poor. You become unstable emotionally and over-react to the normal stresses and strains of everyday living. You "blow a fuse" at the slightest provocation.

Fortunately, except in cases of extreme organic damage, thiamine therapy usually brings dramatic recoveries, even after the deficiency has advanced to the stage of beriberi— the name given to extreme thiamine deficiency many years ago.

Back in the 1890's Dr. Christian Eijkman found he could give chickens polyneuritis (beriberi in man) by restricting them to a diet of polished rice; he could reverse the process and cure them when he fed them the natural unprocessed brown rice. That's a clue to the sneaky cook. *Never, never* use processed rice. Brown rice is inexpensive, easy to prepare, delicious, and rich in the "morale" vitamin.

Some day we, if we live that long, will look back in wonder at the absurdity of the "old dark days of unenlightenment" when food was systematically stripped of the very elements which give it nutrient value. How many packages of white rice are sold for every package of brown? Take a look at the shelves in your supermarket. Notice how much space is given to the many brands of white, processed rice and how little is given to the brown, if, indeed, they stock the brown rice at all.

And rice is not the only thiamine-rich grain to be stripped of its nutrients in processing. True, we are not in the dire position of the rice-dependent people stricken with beriberi. *But the average American diet provides no insurance at all against thiamine deficiency.*

"The cereal grains are good sources [of thiamine]," Dr. Lowenberg says, "but the thiamine is in the germ and outer coatings so that refined cereals such as white rice and flour have lost their thiamine."

There are other factors which contribute to a thiamine deficiency: This vitamin is soluble in water (the more you use in cooking, the more thiamine you lose) and destroyed by high temperatures and by some chemicals including soda, frequently used in the treatment of foods. (Some uninformed cooks put baking soda in vegetables.)

Like all other water soluble vitamins, thiamine-containing foods are not stored in the body. They should be eaten every day. Excess amounts are excreted.

Your body's need for thiamine varies under different circumstances. Dr. Myron Brin, writing in *Newer Methods of Nutritional Biochemistry* (Academic Press, 1967), says we need extra supplies of the vitamin during the use of antibiotics, in the case of severe diarrhea and "in any other situation that would affect adversely the absorption or utilization of the nutrient."

When you are pregnant, or nursing, when you are facing surgery, these are stressful conditions that call for more thiamine. If junior is in training for the football team, sister is trying out for the cheer-leading squad, or, if either has a fever, he needs more thiamine. Any kind of increase in physical activity—starting a gym and swim program—calls for more of this vitamin.

If you are dangling grandchildren on your knee, you need more thiamine than Miss Sweet Sixteen. Intake should increase as birthdays increase. The Committee on Foods and Nutrition of the National Research Council recommends 1.5 milligrams a day for a sedentary man and 2.3 mg. for one who is very active. To make doubly sure, I see to it that my family gets much more than the minimum.

One of the most exciting possibilities concerning thiamine is that *more* than just enough can improve mental ability. In an experiment conducted by Dr. Ruth F. Harrell of the Department of Educational Psychology at Columbia University, two groups of children in an orphanage, ages 9 to 19, were closely matched in age, sex, weight, educational status, and mentality. One group was given a daily tablet containing 2 mg. of thiamine; the other group received a placebo. It was a double-blind experiment—the children, of course, did not know which pills they were receiving, and neither did the investigators who wanted to insure objectivity. This procedure was continued for a year. Only after the results were all in, did Dr. Harrell and her associates match up the testing scores to see how the vitamin group performed compared to the placebo group.

Several categories of tests were used, each designed to measure an aspect of mental response. Both groups were tested at the beginning of the experiment and again at the end, and their percentage of improvement compared with the control group. The group which received the thiamine supplement showed astonishing improvement in all categories—as much as 25 percent to 3200 percent. "It appears," says Drs. E. Cheraskin, W. M. Ringsdorf and J. W. Clark, in *Diet and Disease* (Rodale Books, 1968) "that mental achievement in children of presumably normal diet can be remarkably increased through employment of dietary supplements."

Mental alertness, then, like emotional stability, serenity, an even, pleasant disposition and a zest for living have all been shown to suffer when dietary intake of thiamine is low. With plenty of thiamine, your morale hits new highs and you enjoy that wonderful feeling of being able to cope.

The foods that are rich in thiamine are, of course, also rich in all the other B complex vitamins. You should get your thiamine not separately but as a part of the B complex in a natural compound—brewer's yeast, desiccated liver and wheat germ—*the trio that can change your life.*

Make Sure You Get Magnesium

An undersupply of several other nutrients can alter your personality. If you are even mildly deficient in the mineral magnesium you are apt to be highly nervous, irritable, quick to pick a quarrel, uncooperative, withdrawn, surly, apathetic or belligerent.

Tip to mothers when the children are "impossible": Put out a dish of sunflower seeds, raw almonds or raw cashews —all high in magnesium—where they can't miss them. I don't know whether it's because their jaws are so busy or because the magnesium is going to work, but somehow, this little nutty repast seems to have a magical effect on rambunctious dispositions.

Watch Your Calcium Intake

Calcium helps to control nervous tension and irritability. Whenever you feel the need of a tranquilizer—don't. Take calcium instead—I use the bone meal because it has other minerals that work with the calcium.

Another most common reason for feeling "draggy" all

day is low blood sugar, frequently the price of doing without breakfast. Cutting out breakfast in an effort to lose weight is a big mistake, obviously.

If the children are going to school without breakfast, because they don't know how to make their own and no one is up to make it for them or because they're simply too rushed, get your heads together. Call a meeting of the family council, do something to remedy the situation. Make sure they get a breakfast somehow. And make it a good, high protein meal, including eggs and oatmeal, fruit, and vitamin supplements (see breakfast suggestions), or some other whole grain cereal.

If you can't be with them for breakfast, then teach them how to prepare soft boiled or poached eggs, scrambled eggs, French toast, oatmeal, Wheatena. Don't let them get the dry cereal habit unless they add a big, healthy shot of wheat germ to it. And make sure to stock cereals that have no chemical additives or freshness preservers. These chemicals destroy enzymes. You need every enzyme you can harness. They carry oxygen to your cells. It is very hard to find a commercial dry cereal without additives. Go to a health food store or make your own.

On those days when the children oversleep and just don't have time to prepare a regular breakfast, have them make an all-in-one, vitamin and mineral rich protein drink in the blender, using wheat germ, soy powder, yeast and carob powder in either a raw milk, soy milk or fruit juice base. Experiment till you find the most pleasant mixture and prepare the powdered ingredients ahead of time. Then they have only to add a few tablespoonfuls to the liquid of their choice, blend and drink. Boy, what that does to your spark plugs!

The important thing is to make a hard and fast rule. Breakfast is a *must* even if you are going to be late for school! Better to get to school late full of vim and vigor, than to get there on time, then droop in the middle of the morning.

And there is no doubt at all that you will droop when your blood sugar gets low. Don't make the horrible mistake many people make of eating sweets when your blood sugar is low. Sugar and refined flour products only aggravate low blood sugar. They give you a quick up, then a let-down sets in that leaves you lower than you were before and once more triggers the desire to eat something sweet. It's a vicious circle. *Don't* get caught up in it! Build up your protein stores and your blood sugar won't be apt to act like a yo-yo.

Here are some recipes that will help build morale at your house, improve dispositions and put a new twinkle in every eye.

These patties will provide lots of all the B vitamins and some very important minerals. You can serve them with dinner, between meals as a good pick-up snack, or for breakfast. Make them up the night before but don't griddle or bake them. The next morning, the children can put them in the oven or on the griddle and have a good wholesome breakfast.

Include some form of fresh fruit and a yeast beverage to round it out.

Brown Rice and Carrot Patties

2 cups cooked brown rice	1 egg
½ cup grated carrots	wheat germ and sesame seeds

Mix the rice and carrots to form patties. Dip the patties into the beaten egg, then in wheat germ and sesame seed. Brown on griddle that has been greased well with soy oil over low heat or bake them in the oven on a greased cookie sheet, at 350° until brown.

Gourmet Eggs

Eggs can be not only a nutritious but a very delicious food. Eggs are an excellent source of high quality protein, the B complex vitamins and vitamin A. They also contain vitamins D, E, some K and many minerals. They have saturated fats but they also are rich in both unsaturated fats and lecithin which dissolve cholesterol. Try to get fertile eggs which will give you valuable nutritional substances not available in an infertile egg layed by an old maid chicken who has never known a rooster. A French medical journal, *Compte Rendue de la Société de Biologie* reports a research study by Dr. Riboullearo which showed that fertile eggs contain valuable hormones. Non-fertile eggs don't contain the slightest trace of such hormones.

If you can't get fertile eggs, try to get barnyard eggs from chickens allowed to hunt and peck.

Eggs in the Shell

Boiling water	Eggs at room temperature

Eggs should *never* be boiled. This makes the white hard and rubbery and destroys nutrients. Instead, enough water to cover the eggs completely should be brought to a rapid boil. Then lower the eggs into the water gently with a spoon and reduce the heat so that the water just barely simmers. If you are cooking electrically, you can turn off the heat completely when you lower the eggs into the water. To bring the eggs to room temperature and prevent their cracking when they hit the hot water, place them in a bowl of warm water when you take them out of the refrigerator before you put the water on to boil. You will soon be able to synchronize these steps so that it becomes automatic.

"Soft boiled" or soft cooked eggs should be left in the simmering water for three to four and one-half minutes.

"Hard boiled" or hard cooked eggs should be left in the simmering water for 10 minutes, drained immediately and plunged into cold water to make peeling easier.

Scrambled Eggs and Peppers

6 eggs at room temperature
2 tablespoons water
2 tablespoons soy oil
vegetable seasoning and kelp
  to taste

1 small onion, diced (optional)
1 small green pepper, diced

The secret of turning out a good batch of scrambled eggs is to always cook them over low heat. The very best way to do this is to cook them in the top part of a double boiler over rapidly boiling water. If you use a skillet, use a very low flame. Don't be impatient. They'll cook. The eggs should be well mixed but not overbeaten. They should not be frothy. Use a fork—not an egg beater—to get this effect. Stir in the water and seasoning.

Sauté the diced onion and pepper in the oil over a low flame until they are translucent. Add the beaten eggs and proceed as though making plain scrambled eggs. The eggs should be stirred gently—they should not be "agitated" as is the usual frenzied custom. This recipe makes two to three delicious servings.

Get Up and Go Pancakes

They stick to your ribs and provide morale-boosting B vitamins and protein.

3 eggs
3 tablespoons sunflower seeds

3 tablespoons pumpkin seeds

Beat the eggs well; add the sunflower and pumpkin seeds, which have been ground in seed grinder or crushed with a rolling pin. Cook as for pancakes using about two spoonfuls of batter to each pancake. Serve with honey, pure maple syrup or natural peanut butter.

Polynesian Muffins

4 eggs (separated)
1 cup crushed pineapple (unsweetened)
4 tablespoons cooking oil

2 tablespoons honey
1½ cups yellow cornmeal
½ cup wheat germ flour

Beat the egg whites stiff after blending other ingredients, and then fold into egg yolks gently. Pour into oiled muffin cups. (Using paper cupcake liners saves your pan and the muffins come out easier. But oil the papers if you use them.) Bake at 350° for about 25 minutes.

Egg Croquettes

2 chopped hard cooked eggs
½ cup cooked brown rice
2 tablespoons homemade
  mayonnaise
½ teaspoon grated onion

1 tablespoon water
1½ teaspoons dill seed
soy grits or sesame seeds for
  rolling in

Combine ingredients in order given. Shape into 3 or 4 flat cakes. Roll generously in soy grits which have been crushed a little. Bake on an oiled pan about 10 or 15 minutes until brown.

Old Fashioned Buckwheat Pancakes

½ cup dehydrated whey
1 cup warm water
1 package yeast
1 beaten egg

2 tablespoons cooking oil
1 teaspoon sea salt
½ cup pure buckwheat flour
½ cup wheat germ flour

Dissolve the powdered whey in the warm water, then add the yeast and let stand for 10 minutes. Add the other ingredients, and let stand at room temperature for several hours. Bake. This recipe will make about 10 pancakes.

Corn Chapatties

Here is the famous chapattie of India.

Some people sprinkle them with powdered brewer's yeast, which seems to blend in with the slightly sour but delightful flavor of the chapatties.

2 cups yellow cornmeal
2 tablespoons cooking oil

1½ cups hot water

Pour the hot water over the other ingredients and blend. Shape into thin patties. Bake slowly on a hot griddle or skillet, turning once. The griddle should be slightly oiled and the chapatties allowed to cook slowly on each side.

Wheat Germ Pancakes

2 cups nut milk
4 eggs, separated
2 tablespoons cooking oil
(cold-pressed)

2 teaspoons sea kelp
1 teaspoon honey (optional)
2 cups wheat germ
1 cup brown rice flour

Beat the egg yolks, then add the milk, oil, kelp, honey, wheat germ and flour. Beat well, and fold in the stiffly beaten whites of the 4 eggs just before baking at 350° till nicely browned. This recipe makes about 16 nutritious pancakes, brimming with good health.

Foods Containing the Largest Amounts of Vitamin B₁ (Thiamine)

Foods	Milligrams of Vitamin B_1
Almonds	.25 in 100 almonds
Asparagus, fresh	.16 in 12 stalks
Avocado	.12 in ½ avocado
*Bacon, medium fat	.42 in 12 slices broiled
Barley, whole	.40 in 6 tablespoons
Beans, fresh lima	.25 in ½ cup cooked
Beans, dried lima	.60 in ½ cup cooked
Beef brains	.25 in 2 slices
Beef heart	.54 in 2 slices
Beef, lean	.10 to .13 in average serving
Bran, wheat	.52 in 4 cups
Bread, bakers' whole wheat	.28 in 4 slices
Bread, bakers' light rye	.16 in 4 slices
Brussels sprouts	.11 in 7 sprouts cooked
Cashew nuts	.66 in about 60 nuts
Cauliflower	.09 in ¼ of a small head
Collards	.19 in ½ cup, cooked
Cornmeal, white, whole grain	.41 in 100 grams
Cornmeal, yellow, whole grain	.45 in 100 grams
Crackers, graham	.30 in 10 crackers
Dandelion greens	.19 in 1 cup steamed

Foods	Milligrams of Vitamin B_1
Egg yolk, fresh	.32 in 6 yolks
Farina, enriched	.37 in ½ cup
Figs, dried	.13 in 6 medium figs
Flour, buckwheat	.31 in 100 grams
Flour, rye, whole	.47 in 100 grams
Flour, soy	.82 in 100 grams
Flour, whole wheat	.56 in 100 grams
*Ham, lean, fresh	.96 in 1 slice
*Ham, lean, smoked	.78 in 1 slice
*Ham, picnic	.94 in 1 slice
Hominy	.15 in ½ cup cooked
Kidney, beef	.45 in ½ cup diced
Lamb, leg, roast	.21 in 2 slices
Lentils, dried, split	.73 in 1½ cups
Liver, beef, fresh	.27 in 1 slice
Liver, calf, fresh	.52 in 2 slices
Milk, dried skim	.35 in 10 tablespoons
Milk, dried whole	.30 in 10 tablespoons
Oatmeal, rolled oats	.55 in ¼ cup uncooked
Peanuts, roasted	.30 in 100 peanuts
Peanut butter	.20 in 6 tablespoons
Peas, chick	.35 in 1½ cups cooked
Peas, split	.87 in 1½ cups cooked
Peas, fresh green	.36 in 1 cup cooked
Pecans	.72 in 100 pecans
Plums, fresh	.15 in 2 plums
Pork, lean loin	1.04 in 1 slice
Pork, sausage	.22 in 6 links cooked
Pork, salt	.18 in 1 piece broiled
Pork, spareribs	.92 in 5 pieces cooked
Raisins, seeded	.15 in 1 cup
Rice, brown, unpolished	.29 in ¾ cup steamed
Soy beans	1.14 in ½ cup dried
Turnip greens	.10 in ½ cup steamed
Veal, chops	.18 in 2 medium chops
Veal, cutlet	.18 in 1 slice
Veal, leg roast	.17 in 2 slices

* You will note that I have included the B_1 content of bacon and ham. Please keep in mind that I do not recommend eating either of these foods because of their very high salt content.

Foods Containing the Largest Amounts of Vitamin B_1 (Thiamine)

Foods	Milligrams of Vitamin B_1
Veal, stew meat	.17 in 4 slices
Walnuts, black	.33 in about 100 nuts
Walnuts, English	.48 in about 100 nuts
Wheat, entire	.56 in 10 tablespoons
Wheat bran	.52 in 5 cups
Wheat germ	.68 plus in about 3 tablespoons
Yeast, brewer's	3.23 plus in about 3 tablespoons

Foods Containing the Largest Amounts of Niacin

Foods	Milligrams of Niacin
Almonds	5 in 80 almonds
Beef, fresh chuck	5 in 2 slices
Beef, hamburger	4.3 in 1 hamburger cake
Beef, loin steaks	4.6 in 1 steak
Beef, rib steaks	4.7 in 2 slices
Beef, round steak	5.2 in 1 piece
Beef, rump	4.2 in 2 slices
Beef, soup meat	5.5 in 2-3 pieces
Beef, stew meat	4.3 in 3 pieces
Beef, tongue	5 in 12 slices
Buckwheat	4 in 100 grams
Chicken	8.6 in 3 slices
Fish, medium fat	4.2 in 1 piece
Flour, whole wheat	5.6 in 100 grams
Fresh ham	4.1 in 1 slice
Heart, beef	6.8 in 2 slices
Heart, pork	8 in 2 slices
Kidney, beef	10 in ½ cup cubed
Lamb, leg roast	5.9 in 2 slices
Lamb, shoulder roast	5.2 in 4 slices
Lamb, sirloin chops	5.9 in 2 chops
Lentils, dried	3 in 1½ cups cooked
Liver, fresh	16.1 in 1 piece
Mackerel, Atlantic	5.8 in ½ cup
Mackerel, Pacific	8.7 in ½ cup
Mushrooms	6 in 7 mushrooms
Peanut butter	16.2 in 5 tablespoons
Peanuts, roasted	16.2 in 100 peanuts
Pork, Boston butt	4.5 in 1 slice
Pork, loin	4.4 in 1 slice
Pork, spareribs	3.9 in 4 pieces
Rice, brown	4.6 in ¾ cup
Salmon	7.4 in 1 piece
Swordfish	9.1 in 1 piece

Foods	Milligrams of Niacin
Turkey	7.9 in 2 slices
Veal, chops	6.3 in 2 medium chops
Veal, cutlet	6.4 in 1 slice
Veal, roast	6.3 in 2 slices
Veal, stew meat	6 in 4 slices
Wheat bran	32 in 4 cups
Wheat germ	4.6-7 in 12 tablespoons
Yeast, brewer's	9.5 in 3 tablespoons

Foods Containing the Largest Amounts of Pantothenic Acid

Foods	Pantothenic Acid Content in Milligrams
Artichokes, Jerusalem	.40 in 4 artichokes
Barley	1.0 in 7 tablespoons
Beans, dried navy or lima	.83 in ½ cup
Beef, brain	1.8 in 2 pieces
Beef, heart	2.0 in 2 pieces
Beef, liver	5.2 in 1 piece
Beef, lean	1.0 in 1 piece
Broccoli	1.4 in 1 cup
Carrots	.2 in ½ cup
Cauliflower	.92 in ¼ head
Cheese	.96 in five 1-inch cubes
Chicken	.90 in 3 slices
Corn	.31 in ½ cup
Cowpeas	2.1 in 1½ cups
Egg, whole fresh	2.7 in 2 eggs
Egg, yolk	6.3 in 8 yolks
Lamb, leg	.81 in 2 slices
Kale	.30 in 1 cup
Milk, fresh whole	.29 in ½ cup
Milk, skim	.36 in ½ cup
Mushrooms	1.7 in 7 mushrooms
Oats, rolled	1.3 in ¾ cup
Oranges	.49 in 1 medium orange
Oysters	.49 in 5 medium oysters
Peas, fresh	.60 in 1 cup
Peas, dried	2.8 in 1½ cups
Peanuts, roasted	2.5 in 100 peanuts
Potatoes, Irish	.65 in 1 medium potato
Potatoes, sweet	.95 in 1 medium potato
Pork, bacon	.98 in 25 slices*
Pork, ham	.66 in 1 slice*
Pork, muscle	1.5 in 1 piece*
Rice, polished	.40 in ¾ cup

Foods	Pantothenic Acid Content in Milligrams
Rice, bran	2.20 in ¾ cup
Salmon	1.1 in ½ cup
Soybeans	1.8 in ½ cup
Strawberries	.26 in ½ cup
Walnuts, English	.80 in 100 walnuts
Wheat, whole	1.3 in ½ cup
Wheat, bran	3.0 in 5 cups
Wheat germ	1.0 in 6 tablespoons
Yeast, brewer's	10.0 in 3 tablespoons
Zucchini	.30 in ½ cup

Chapter X

When Happiness Was
A Pocketful of Polly Seeds

Back in depression days, when we were counting pennies instead of calories, happiness was a pocketful of polly seeds.

They were known as polly seeds because poll parrots loved them. Today, they are known as sunflower seeds. In those days, every Russian immigrant would fill his pockets with these delicious, nutty morsels before he went to work or out for a walk. And no matter how heavy hearted or overburdened, somehow a pocketful of polly seeds and a friend to share them had the effect of making one's pack of troubles a little lighter.

This polly seed habit is well worth reviving. For one thing, if you are a smoker, the seeds in the shell keep your hands and mouth so busy, you don't get a chance to reach for the cigarette. If you're a snacker, fighting the battle of the bulge, you can munch happily and in good conscience and consume a negligible number of calories.

71

But, perhaps, the good feeling that came with the polly seeds was due to the fact that seeds are storehouses for many of the elements that promote a feeling of well-being. Seeds have what it takes to turn you on—and no side effects!

A seed is, when you stop to think about it, the very core of life. It contains, within its tiny kernel, a mysterious, fantastic concentration of energy and nutrients designed by Nature, the master chemist, to get the plant up and keep it growing. This core of life in seeds brings a quality of liveliness to those who eat them.

Consider what a powerhouse of nutrition you get in a pocketful of polly seeds: Seeds are a remarkable source of the unsaturated fatty acids, vitamin F, so very hard to get into our diets, since oils are almost all refined today. Sunflowers are especially high in precious linoleic acid, an essential fatty acid which helps to prevent harmful deposits of cholesterol, providing protection against such diseases as arteriosclerosis, kidney stones and gall bladder stones.

We need vitamin F—the essential fatty acids—not only to protect us from debilitating conditions, but for smooth, beautiful skin and healthy hair. During the winter, when skin and hair tends to become dry, I put a dish of polly seeds out along with the raw vegetables just before dinner. According to eminent English nutritionist, Dr. Hugh Sinclair, we need vitamin F for the prevention of bronchial asthma, rheumatoid arthritis and ulcers. When there is a sheaf of bills in the mail, I make sure there's a dish of polly seeds smack on top of them. We need it to improve our resistance to all diseases because it helps to build strong connective tissue in the cells. We need it especially for normal reproductive processes and normal healthy reproductive organs. When we went to pay a call on a friend recuperating from a miscarriage, we did not bring a box of candy. We brought a vacuum sealed can of sunflower seeds —done up with red ribbon.

Vitamin E—you get as much as 31 units of vitamin E in every 3½ ounces of seeds and 222 units of total tocopherols. Vitamin E, as you know, is absolutely essential for smooth functioning of all reproductive processes, for heart and muscle health, and is a superb preventive of internal blood clots.

Vitamin B's—(thiamine, riboflavin, niacin). It is not generally known, but sunflower seeds contain more of the vitamin B complex than an equivalent quantity of wheat germ. In 100 grams of sunflower seeds you would get as much as 5.8 milligrams of niacin, 1.96 milligrams of thiamine and .23 milligrams of riboflavin. Investigators find that they can use sunflower seeds as the only source of the B vitamins in the diet of various animals. When the children get the nail-biting jitters over exams, I put a big dish of seeds on their desks or in the middle of the kitchen table. It sure improves their dispositions. They call it survival food.

Since refined sugar and flour, smoking, and drinking of alcoholic beverages rob your stores of the B vitamins, it might be wise to prepare your body against the ravages of a night of socializing with a pocketful of polly seeds.

Zinc—one of the trace minerals that triggers the action of many enzymes and vitamins. Dr. Walter Pories, a pioneer in zinc research, once dubbed zinc "the mineral for men" because it is vital to the development of the sex glands of men.

Magnesium—because of processing, this mineral is deficient in a great many diets. Magnesium is the mineral that helps you see the silver lining behind every cloud. It is absolutely essential to the formation of strong blood vessels and bones, and nerves that can take it. Perhaps no other food packs so much of this essential nutrient into so small a package. When you notice that spirits are getting glum, get out the sunflower seeds.

Pectin—this substance may offer valuable protection against the accumulation of strontium 90 in the body. Russian researchers say that the addition of pectin from sunflowers to the diet of animals "binds radioactive strontium in the gastrointestinal tracts and reduces the absorption and deposition of the isotopes in the skeleton." It has been known for more than 100 years that the ingestion of pectin prevents lead poisoning.

And that's not all you get with your pectin insurance policy. Professor Ancel Keys, director of the Laboratory of Physical Hygiene of the University of Minnesota and a noted research scientist, has been pointing out in recent years that pectin has a beneficial effect on the blood cholesterol level.

Vitamin A—essential for a beautiful complexion, for good eyesight and for the health of your mucous membrane. *The Agricultural Handbook of the Composition of Foods* credits the sunflower seed with 50 I. U. of easily-assimilated vitamin A to every 100 grams of sunflower seed kernels.

Protein—it would seem that sunflower seeds have all this

and heaven, too. Besides their rich content of minerals and vitamins, sunflower seeds are high in methionine, an amino acid which is usually lacking in vegetable foods, and the ten essential amino acids not usually found in nutritious amounts in any food but meat and fish. Whenever the children bring an unexpected guest to dinner, I stretch the protein of the main dish with sunflower seeds. Put a half a cup of seeds in the chow mein or put a dish of them on the table and let them add their own.

Vitamin D—the most difficult vitamin to obtain in the diet. Very few foods contain it. It is not even listed on most charts of food values. Sunflower seeds are a good source of vitamin D, which they form in such large amounts because they are exposed to the ultra violet rays from the sun for long periods of time, since their faces turn to the sun from its rising to its setting. Particularly valuable, this vitamin D, which governs the formation and integrity of bone tissue, comes with those minerals which work with vitamin D to promote the health of the teeth and bones—calcium, magnesium, silicon, fluorine, phosphorus, etc. Without these minerals, vitamin D cannot do its work.

Minerals—Sunflower seeds are an excellent source of essential minerals, including the important trace minerals lacking in most foods, even vegetables and fruits. But the sunflower is a voracious mineral feeder. Its roots go down deep to draw up trace minerals not ordinarily present in the topsoil. One of these is fluorine, a mineral lacking in most soils, which is essential to protect the enamel of the teeth.

Enzymes—so vital are enzymes to life itself that some scientists define life as an orderly functioning of enzymes. All vital processes in cells are initiated and fulfilled by enzymes. But enzymes are as fragile as they are vital. They are easily inhibited, disorganized, or even destroyed by physical and chemical agents, disinfectants, preservatives and many drugs in common use; some are destroyed by temperatures only a little higher than that of the human body.

As we cook our food in order to make it digestible or more appetizing, we inactivate or destroy many of our enzymes. We need uncooked food in order to have complete enzyme systems. This is the advantage offered by the sunflower seed. Since it can be eaten and enjoyed raw, all its beneficial properties are realized.

Take advantage of the tremendous benefits of sunflower seeds: eat them just slightly toasted as the Russians do, or added to salads, baked goods, or wherever you would use nuts. You can use sunflower seed meal, which mixes well with other flours and is ideal for making pastry. It is useful, too, for thickening sauces, gravies and soups. Added to water and whizzed in the blender, the meal makes a delightful seed milk which can be used in place of cow's milk. Here's another way to make seed milk suggested by Frieda Nusz in her cookbook *Wheat and Sugar Free*.

½ cup sunflower seeds   3 soft cooked eggs
½ cup sesame seeds

Put everything in blender and add hot water gradually until thick and smooth. Keep adding water to thin and when blender is full, pour into jar and add enough water to make 4 or 5 cups of milk. Sunflower alone is the mildest tasting. Use all sunflower seeds for sunflower seed milk.

The most economical way to keep your pockets full of polly seeds is to buy the kind that are packaged for the birds. Wash them in a colander—then spread on a cookie sheet and dry them in a very slow oven (100°) for about an hour. Don't roast them. This destroys the valuable enzymes.

We like to use the seeds in the shell when we sit around the fire at night swapping stories, when we go for walks and sometimes after dinner when we want to linger over dessert.

I put little packs of the shelled seeds in the children's lunch boxes and in my husband's pocket. They take the edge off the impulse that makes you reach for candy or coffee.

I use the sunflower meal in almost everything I bake. It gives a delightful nutty taste that everyone enjoys.

Not only sunflower but all seeds are rich in nutrients.

Pumpkin seeds are 30% protein, rich in iron, calcium, phosphorous and zinc. Use them for snacking, mixed with sunflower seeds. Use them whenever you would use nuts.

Sesame seeds are 45% protein, rich in polyunsaturates that are so good for the heart and blood vessels. Use Tahini (sesame seed butter) as a spread, in halvah, with chick peas and a smidgeon of garlic to make humus—a delicious spread popular in the Middle East. Use sesame seeds as a coating wherever you would be apt to use breadcrumbs.

Sunflower Seed Content

Approximate analysis per 100 grams or about ¼ pound of sunflower seeds

Minerals

Iron	6.0 mgs.
Phosphorus	860.0 mgs.
Calcium	57.0 mgs.
Iodine	0.07 mg.
Magnesium	347.0 mgs.
Potassium	630.0 mgs.
Manganese	25 parts per million
Copper	20 parts per million

B-Vitamins

B_1 (Thiamine)	2.2	mgs.
B_2 (Riboflavin)	0.28	mg.
Niacin	5.6	mgs.
B_6 (Pyridoxine)	1.1	mgs.
Para-Amino-Benzoic Acid	62.	mgs.
Biotin	0.067	mg.
Choline	216.00	mgs.
Inositol	147.00	mgs.
Folic Acid	0.1	mg.
Pantothenic Acid	2.2	mgs.
Pantothenol	3.5	mgs.

Other Vitamins

Vitamin D	92 U.S.P. Units
Vitamin E	31 International Units
Protein	25%
Sunflower Oil	48.44% (over 90% unsaturated acids)

Chapter XI

Get Smart—Use Brains

I have never seen "brains" on the menu in any restaurant. Have you? Perhaps they call them sweetbreads. The two are similar in appearance and texture and are interchangeable in recipes. But they are different—nutritionally. While sweetbreads (thymus) is a good food, brains are far superior in some nutrients and give you fewer than half the calories measure for measure.

Besides being a wonderful source of protein, of the most superior quality, brains are one of the richest sources of the B vitamin, choline, which plays an important role in the utilization of cholesterol in the body. So—the smart thing to do is to use brains—they're good for your heart.

This is easier said than done. Is there anyone who does not recoil emotionally at the very thought of eating brains? How does the sneaky cook meet this challenge?

77

No Peeking Please

The smart sneaky cook puts brains in the soup—when the pot peekers are far away from the kitchen. My son once lifted the lid and wanted to know *who* I was cooking for dinner. Most of the brainy nutrients will go into the soup. (B vitamins are water soluble.) After the brain has enriched the soup, you should do one of two things—either take it out and use it later in chopped meat dishes or put it through the blender with some of the vegetables and broth. The idea is to disguise it. If there are no protests, take another brainy step. Cook the brains in a small amount of water and use both the broth and the brain in chopped liver and chopped meat recipes. You can go creative with brains and make a spread that tastes just like chopped herring. I call it the Get Smart Appetizer.

Ingredients:
1 set pre-cooked brains
1 tart apple
½ chopped onion

1 hard-cooked egg
a little wine vinegar or juice from a jar of pickled herring

Combine all ingredients in wooden chopping bowl. Chop to smooth spreadable consistency. Arrange in glass serving dish, top with sesame seeds and serve as a dip with raw vegetables, rye krisp, or homemade crackers.

Here are some more wonderful ways to use brains. I learned most of these from my mother.

Fried Calf's Brains

1 set calf's brains
Cold water to cover
1 clove garlic

4 tablespoons oil
¼ cup wheat germ
Sea salt and paprika

Scald brains. Drain. Remove membrane. Add cold water to cover and a cut clove of garlic. Cook over moderate heat 20 minutes. Drain. When cool enough to handle, slice into ½ inch thick pieces. Heat frying pan over a moderate heat. Add oil. Dip each slice of brains in wheat germ and sauté till nicely browned on both sides. Dust with salt and paprika. Serve hot. (Serves 2)

Brains with Scrambled Eggs

1 set calf's brains
Boiling water to cover
¼ cup soy flour mixed with 1 tablespoon sesame seeds
4 tablespoons oil

3 eggs
Pinch of sea salt
3 slices toast
2 tablespoons minced parsley

Scald brains and drain. Remove membrane and cut into ½ inch thick cubes. Roll in flour and sauté till nicely browned. Beat eggs slightly and add salt. Pour over fried brains, reduce heat, cover and let cook 20 minutes. Uncover, stir with a fork to break up into small pieces. Cover toast with the brains and scrambled eggs and top with minced parsley. Instead of toast, try this on brown rice for a nice change. (Serves 3)

Brain Fritters

1 set calf's brains	¼ cup soy flour
Cold water to cover	3 tablespoons cold water
2 tablespoons vinegar	Pinch of sea salt and paprika
½ teaspoon sea salt	Hot oil for sautéeing
2 eggs	

Cook brains in water with vinegar and sea salt 25 to 30 minutes over moderate heat. Drain. Remove membrane. Slice ¼ inch thick. Beat eggs, stir in flour and cold water to make a thick batter. Add salt and paprika and beat 2 or 3 strokes. Dip sliced brains in batter and fry in hot oil till nicely browned on both sides. (Serves 2 to 3)

Brains with Egg Sauce

1 set beef or calf's brains	Dash of ginger
Boiling water to cover	2 eggs
1 onion, diced or sliced thin	2 tablespoons lemon juice
1 green pepper, diced	1 tablespoon cornstarch or
1 tomato, diced	arrowroot starch
1 cup hot water	1 tablespoon cold water
¼ teaspoon sea salt and paprika	

Cover brains with boiling water and cook for 5 minutes. Drain. Remove membrane. Place brains, uncut, in a saucepan and add vegetables, hot water, salt, paprika and ginger. Cover and cook over moderate heat 30 to 35 minutes. Lift out brains and put the sauce through a coarse strainer. There should be about 1 cup of sauce. Return sauce to saucepan and stir in well-beaten eggs and lemon juice. Blend cornstarch with cold water and add. Cook over low heat, stirring till smooth. Add the brains and cover. Simmer 10 minutes. (Serves 2 to 3)

Chapter XII

Change Your Sex Life
Without Changing Partners

"Dear Abby: George and I have been married only nine years. I am 29 and George is 30, so we can't be considered 'old.' But listen to this: Last night I was feeling in a romantic mood, so I put the stereo on, bathed, combed my hair real pretty, and put on my best nightie and his favorite cologne. I snuggled up close to him and whispered, 'George, I'm chilly.' Do you know what he said? 'Turn up the electric blanket!' What would you have done?—Karen"

"Dear Karen," replied Dear Abby. "I'd have turned up the electric blanket."

If Karen is smart, she won't settle for a blanket to give her the kind of electricity that every woman craves. No matter how hot the blanket, it's never been a magic carpet that lands you on the moon.

If Karen is smart and wants the full expression of her husband's love, she will seek out the real cause for his lack of sexual response. She may well find that it has nothing to do with gossamer nighties and sensuous colognes.

Along with many so-called "love-starved women," Karen may well find that the wine of sex, that makes for romance in the bedroom, is brewed in the kitchen.

Karen might think, "Well, what could I possibly do in the kitchen to improve his nutrition? I give him a balanced diet and he eats like a horse." George could eat like two horses and never get a decent amount of vitamin E because it's practically eliminated from the American diet by the way our grains and oils are refined.

Vitamin E is vitally important, but it's only one of the nutrients that can bring that "ole black magic" into the bedroom. There are many more, and Karen can provide them by cleverly substituting live foods for devitalized ones. A subtle change of snacks can furnish the elements glands need for secreting certain hormones. These are basic to the health and vitality of the whole complex system that culminates in what is, for many, the most perfect and satisfying experience in human life.

While bedroom fatigue is becoming more widespread among men, it is not exclusive to the male of the species. The same kitchen magic we shall outline for *him* applies to *her*. It can make a whale of a difference that swings her from a "not tonight, dear, I'm too tired" reaction to one of excitement and anticipation for an act of love she'll make sure she's never too tired to enjoy.

In order to work this kind of magic in the kitchen, you must understand something about your glands and how to nourish them.

You may not know it, but your glands working behind the scenes have more influence than your mother-in-law.

Endocrine glands—these mysterious chemical laboratories—hold the secret of your sexual power, your desire for sex and your ability to produce. The hormones and other secretions produced by these glands, Dr. Paavo Airola says in *Sex and Nutrition* (Information Inc., New York, 1970), are the spark plugs that trigger and stimulate not only your sexual activity but dramatically affect your general well-being, both physically and mentally.

Testosterone, the male sex hormone, and estrogen, the female hormone, are as important to your sex life as to your general health. These hormones and other secretions of the endocrine glands provide stimulus and drive for the body as well as the mind. The healthy function of the endocrine glands and sufficient production of hormones are indispensable to healthy functioning of the sex organs.

It's as simple as that.

What do your glands need to be healthy? They need specific minerals and vitamins to function properly. Adulterated, refined foods—the usual fare in the American home—cannot possibly provide these nutrients. On the contrary, the chemical additives which most of our food is bathed in not only contribute to the destruction of health, they are turning our men into sexual weaklings, Dr. Airola maintains. "Our diet habits relate to an increase in the number of miscarriages and an increase in the number of birth defects. Few of us realize how powerful is the effect of malnutrition on the organs of *reproduction*."

So glands are the fountainhead of your sex life. Take the thyroid which most people associate with weight problems. True, an insufficient secretion of thyroid hormone, thyroxin, slows down metabolic rate and contributes to obesity. But the consequences go much farther. No matter how fancy your nightgown, you can't be really sensuous when you have an underactive thyroid, nor can you hope to inspire a true desire for sex in a hypothyroid man. A weak or lazy thyroid can turn a young vital man into an old man who, when he gets into bed wants to sleep—period.

Nutritional deficiencies sometimes responsible for an underactive thyroid are iodine and the B vitamins, especially B_1. When you're in the mood for love, serve a delicious Chinese dinner. Season the chow mein with kelp for iodine and serve it on brown rice for lots of B_1. It wouldn't hurt to think lovely thoughts.

Many people seeking the road to a more exciting sex life through a sexier figure, go on weight reducing diets that eliminate oils. They lose weight all right. They also lose the mood for love. Persons on seemingly adequate diets, except for oil, have reported increased sex interest after oil was added to their dietary, says nutritionist Adelle Davis. To lose weight sensibly, don't cut out oils. You need them.

Because the thyroid gland controls the speed at which all body activities occur, an undersupply of thyroid hormone results in fatigue, lethargy, a feeling of coldness, loss of interest in sex and a tendency to gain weight rapidly on few calories.

When a deficiency already exists, more iodine is needed. It is important to remember that there are substances in peanuts, untoasted soy flour and vegetables of the cabbage family which combine with iodine and prevent it from reaching the blood. This increases the iodine requirement. Four milligrams of iodine daily, the amount in a teaspoon of kelp, is considered adequate to correct thyroid abnormalities.

How do you know when your thyroid gland is not functioning normally? Besides a decrease in libido, if you suffer irregular or profuse menstruation, chronic fatigue, inability to concentrate, headaches, mental sluggishness and unjustified fears and worries, you should suspect a thyroid deficiency and begin to feed that important gland properly.

Make sure you're getting all the B-vitamins you need, especially B_1. Some of your best sources are wheat germ, brewer's yeast, liver, whole grains, nuts, beans and brown rice. For a good source of iodine, use kelp instead of salt. Since vitamin E improves iodine absorption and helps an underactive thyroid gland to produce hormones, iodine and E should be taken together. Put some wheat germ oil in a glass of tomato juice and spike it with a generous dash of kelp to get the combination. With this kind of cocktail, you won't need candlelight and wine.

You've got to have a healthy pituitary for a satisfactory sex life.

The pituitary gland, small but mighty, located at the base of the brain, is the master gland of the endocrine system— the big boss. The hormones manufactured by "little pit" control the functioning of all other endocrine glands, including the sex glands. One of these hormones stimulates the production of milk during nursing.

If your pituitary gland is not working up to par, your sex organs will not mature. It is under the stimulus of the pituitary that the testes produce spermatozoa and male sex hormones, and the ovaries produce ova and female sex hormones. An under-functioning of the pituitary can bring about premature menopause, premature aging of the sex organs and premature impotence in the man in your life.

Even though the pituitary is not considered a sex gland, its influence on the sexual organs and their functions is so profound that its health deserves prime consideration in the kitchen.

Vitamin E lives in the pituitary gland, where it is more concentrated than in any other part of the body, and serves as a protector for both pituitary and adrenal hormones. It prevents their destruction by conserving oxygen. So be sure to sneak some wheat germ oil into the salad dressing—2 teaspoons to a cruet of Italian dressing; 1 teaspoon to a 4 ounce glass of Russian dressing.

The pituitary, adrenal, and sex hormones are all made

from cholesterol, but without pantothenic acid, vitamin A and B vitamins, cholesterol cannot be replaced in the glands once it has been used up. Your best sources for this vitamin as well as all the other members of the B family are brewer's yeast and liver. Along with wheat germ and cold-pressed oils—corn, safflower and sunflower oils—sunflower seeds and sesame seeds are a wonderful source of vitamin E. They also have plenty of the B's and protein. Serve liver coated with sesame seeds and wheat germ and your sex hormones will stand up and march.

In spite of the tremendous ballyhoo about birth control, there are over ten million childless American couples who long for a baby. For centuries infertility has been attributed to the wife. At the World Congress of Fertility and Sterility, held in Stockholm in 1967, it was reported that as much as 50 percent of the time the husband is the infertile partner in a childless marriage.

"It is frustrating to explain the absent or diminished fertility of so many healthy-appearing males and this infertility is on the increase," wrote Dr. M. Leopold Brody in the *Weiss Memorial Hospital Bulletin,* November, 1963. "There are more than 5 million infertile husbands in the U.S. and a much higher number who are only marginally fertile. The reason is a mystery."

Some clues to the mystery are emerging—notably the deficiency of zinc in the usual American diet.

The importance of the trace element, zinc, to virility was dramatically demonstrated in a study by Dr. A. A. Prasad who found that 40 boys admitted to the research ward of the U.S. Naval Medical Research Unit in Cairo, U.A.R., suffered both growth retardation and hypogonadism (retarded genital development). Testing revealed that while iron supplementation and an improved diet aided growth, it was the zinc supplementation which promoted the greatest degree of sex maturation.

It is not only the increasing rate of infertility but another problem which is dimming the enchantment of more and more marriages—the growing lack of sexual spark among young men in their prime who are complaining furtively of "bedroom fatigue."

It used to be that "Not tonight, dear, I'm too tired," was strictly from the girls. But, now more and more young men, because they find themselves poor sexual performers, are turning up their electric blankets.

How does the trace mineral, zinc, affect male performance and potency? Indeed, there is a very high concentration of zinc in the whole male reproductive system, prostate, seminal fluid, and especially in the sperm which contains the highest concentration of zinc of any cell in the human body.

Granted, then, that zinc is a necessary element to fertility and to male performance in the bedroom. Is it more lacking in our diets now than in the days when a man was a man?

Don't meat and potatoes, vegetables and bread, these staples of the American diet, contain the element that contributes to the music of sex? Hardly. Let's look at the record. Like every other mineral element, zinc is concentrated in the bran and germ portion of the cereal grains, removed in the refining.

Meats, vegetables and fruits at one time were a good source of zinc, but Dr. Andre Voisin, in his book, *Soil, Grass and Cancer,* says that part of the deficiency of zinc in the modern diet is due to the fact that modern farming methods with their use of artificial fertilizers and poisonous insecticides have caused a reduction of the amount of zinc in our food plants, which deficiency transmits itself to the cattle and other animals we are consuming.

As with all trace elements, there is an optimum level of zinc. It is possible to get too much or too little. The best way to get all your trace elements in proper balance is from natural unprocessed foods, preferably grown on organically enriched soils.

Nuts and green vegetables are good sources of zinc— especially if they are grown on good soil. However, zinc is easily lost if cooking water is discarded. It is easily lost, too, when excess liquids, particularly alcohol, are consumed, or if any form of diuretic is being used.

Because seeds contain all the elements necessary to launch and sustain a new life, they are rich in the substance so necessary to new life—zinc. Pumpkin seeds, sunflower seeds, sesame seeds are therefore excellent sources of zinc. Serve a dish of mixed seeds and raisins for dessert and TV snack. Herring is rich in zinc. Try chopped herring as an appetizer. So are liver, mushrooms, onions, maple syrup and fertile eggs.

Tomorrow try this herring and potato bake. It's a Russian dish.

Baked Herring and Potato

(zinc rich)

4 medium potatoes	2 ounces oil
3 pickled herrings	salt
¼ pint sour cream or yogurt	paprika
4 ounces wheat germ	

Bake the potatoes in their skins, peel and cut into thin slices. Chop the herrings into fine pieces. Oil an ovenproof dish. Fill it with alternate layers of herrings, and the potatoes, beginning and ending with a layer of potatoes. Spread each layer with sour cream or yogurt and season. Top with wheat germ and dot with oil. Bake in a moderate oven for 40 minutes. (Serves 4)

If you're feeling amorous, and looking forward to a night of love, don't serve hot dogs, or any other food heavy in nitrates, for dinner. In fact, you'd be wise to eliminate them for a sex-happy diet. Frankfurters and all preserved meats are loaded with nitrates and nitrites. And what nitrates and nitrites do to sexuality, you will comprehend better when you realize that another name for potassium nitrate is saltpeter, the substance that was, at one time, sprinkled on the food of prisoners in order to stifle sexual desire.

Vitamin C can be another valuable ally in your program to partake fully of the elixir of human life. A Japanese doctor, M. Higuchi, has demonstrated a relationship between vitamin C levels and the hormone production of the sex glands. Prostatic fluid, which nourishes the sperm and keep them alive, is extremely rich in vitamin C. How about rose hip soup to get your motor going tonight?

Rose hips are the red or orange berries left after the rose petals have fallen. Jean Gordon tells us in her little book, *The Art of Cooking with Rose Hips* (Walker & Co., N.Y.: 1968), that scientific analysis has found rose hips to be 24 to 36 times richer in vitamin C than fresh orange juice and 60 times richer than lemons. Try this recipe for powdered rose hip soup:

2 tablespoons of rose hip powder	2 cups boiling water
	2 tablespoons honey
1 tablespoon soy flour	2 tablespoons of cream

Mix the rose hip powder and flour in a little cold water until smooth. Gradually stir in boiling water. Boil until the mixture thickens, stirring constantly. Add honey and take from the stove. When cold, stir in the cream.

Whenever you bake, add a tablespoon of rose hip powder to a cup of flour. This will give additional nutrition and a nice flavor to muffins, cakes, cookies and pancakes. One tablespoon of rose hip powder mixed with a half cup of date sugar is delicious to sprinkle on cereal or on toast in place of the usual cinnamon and sugar.

You can gather your own rose hips if you have unsprayed bushes. Carefully pick them over, remove the ends and pack them into glass jars and freeze them whole. Take them out of the freezer, make them into a puree and add to juices or just plain water with a little honey added for a delicious beverage, rich in vitamin C.

Vitamin A has a beneficial effect in maintaining testicular tissue in a healthy state. It also goes to bat to help your liver detoxify poisons. Best sources of vitamin A are egg yolk, halibut-liver oil, cod liver oil, liver and organ meats.

All of the B vitamins influence the production of testosterone, the male sex hormone produced by the interstitial cells of the testes.

Now that you know what to add to your diet, it is important to know, too, what to subtract. The nitrate loaded foods and devitalized foods we have already earmarked as the enemies of a happy sex life. Another enemy is tobacco. *The Encyclopedia of Sex Practice* (Wehman Brothers, Hackensack, New Jersey), says that "There have been cases in which potency could only be restored when cigarette smoking was given up altogether."

In women, the "pill" is frequently the cause of sexual frigidity and loss of libido, according to Dr. Airola.

Since the beginning of time, man has sought remedies and foods for enhancing his sexual prowess. The Bible refers to mandrake root. In ancient Babylon women ate halvah to enhance their sex appeal.

A French doctor's research a few years ago gave scientific support to some of the old folklore. The ingredients of halvah, sesame seeds and honey are rich in the vitamins and minerals needed by your glands. Honey is rich in the amino acid, aspartic acid. A doctor in New Jersey has used similar ingredients to treat hundreds of women with what he terms "the housewife syndrome" or chronic fatigue and lack of interest in lovemaking. As many as 87 percent of his patients responded with a startling change in attitude.

While the "sexual revolution" of the last few years is changing attitudes toward sex, most of the research done so far has explored sex problems from a psychological viewpoint. As a result, many couples go to psychiatrists, spend huge sums of money and lots of time digging into their childhood memories while reclining on separate couches. If their diets were improved and their glands and muscles were in really tiptop shape, chances are that 5 minutes on the same couch would solve all their problems beautifully.

Chapter XIII

Darling, Your Deficiencies Are Showing

The night Marjorie J. poured at a swank country club tea in eastern Pennsylvania, she was resplendent in mink, jewels, Chanel No. 5, and a brand new size 7 figure.

"Darling, you look positively smashing," one guest told her. "I wish I had the will power to take off a few bulges." The other women murmured agreement, admiration, and more compliments.

No one, but absolutely no one, came forth and whispered in the ear of the gorgeous Mrs. J., "Darling, your deficiencies are showing!"

And yet every time the lovely Marjorie handed out a cup of refreshment, there was a twitch in her lower eyelid and a slight tremor in her hand. To the knowing eye, Mrs. J.'s deficiencies were as conspicuous as her jewels and overshadowed the allure of her new figure.

You might wonder how a wealthy woman could develop a deficiency severe enough to rattle the tea cups. Certainly she could afford the very best foods available. Certainly she could afford the counsel of top medical men.

Certainly. But Mrs. J., you remember, had been trying to squeeze into a size 7. In order to accomplish this, she went on a popular high protein diet. She did not know that the more protein you eat, the more vitamin B6 and magnesium you need. Both elements are used up in metabolizing of the proteins. Mrs. J. was aware of that tremor. She figured it was nerves and was taking tranquilizers in an effort to control it. No one told her that a need for more vitamin B6 can trigger a tic, a twitch, or a tremor in your hands.

Something else happening to Mrs. J. was also vaguely disturbing to her. It was something she could not put into words. She no longer felt "in harmony." She was nervous, irritable, restless. She found herself reprimanding the children too frequently, speaking with a shrill note of sarcasm that she really didn't intend. When one of the kids poked his head into her room and yelled "Mom," she nearly jumped out of her skin. She jumped every time the phone rang or a door slammed. She wasn't sleeping well. She avoided dark colored clothes these days, because, though she had changed her shampoo and even her hairdresser, she was terribly embarrassed by dandruff flakes she just couldn't control.

When Mrs. J. went on her high protein reducing diet, she was careful to take a vitamin supplement, a highly-touted one-a-day that was widely advertised but neither vitamin B6 nor magnesium were included in the manufacturer's formula.

The night Mrs. J. poured at the country club social she looked much thinner, but felt much worse, than she had six months ago when she started on her diet. If only a friend had whispered in her ear, "Darling, your deficiencies are showing."

He might have told her that she could get magnesium in bone meal and all the B vitamins she needed in foods like brewer's yeast, bananas, wheat germ, soya, blackstrap molasses, beef liver, unpolished rice and sunflower seeds. He would have been helping her to avoid further, more serious complications—anemia, kidney stones, arteriosclerosis.

The case of Mrs. J. is not unique. There are a million carbon copies of her—women and men, too, who travel the rocky road from doctor to tranquilizer to more medication to more side effects and to more misery because they do not recognize the deficiencies that show.

Learn how to recognize your deficiencies and you can have your good health and a superb figure, too. They march in the same parade. Here is a guide which may help you to pinpoint yours and head them off at the pass.

Your deficiencies are showing:
If you tire easily;
If you are irritable;
If you lack enthusiasm;
If you are forgetful;
If you are having aching and tenderness of the calf muscles;
If you feel mentally and physically inadequate;
If your heartbeat is excessively rapid;
If your legs swell;
If you lack appetite;
If you sometimes feel like you're going crazy;
If you just can't stand noisy children;
If you are always tired but can't sleep.

You may need more thiamine (B_1).

Bear in mind that the more sugar and refined flour products you eat, the less thiamine you are getting and the *more you need*.

You must have an adequate supply of thiamine if you are to marshal the energy in your food. Without it, carbohydrates cannot be properly utilized by the body. That is one good reason why you can eat enough to get fat, but still never have any get-up-and-go.

Keep a list of thiamine-rich foods handy in your kitchen. When you plan your menu, check it to make sure you have included several good sources of this "morale" vitamin.

Good sources of thiamine are brown rice, nutritional yeast (use it in soups and stews) and sunflower seeds. Eat them out of hand or put them in salads, cookies and chow mein.

When my husband is in the throes of tax returns, when the kids are in training for the swim team or struggling with finals, I serve chow mein and load it with sneaky ammunition. I frequently invite run-down, depressed or menopausal friends to chow mein dinner and charge their batteries when they're not looking. Here's my recipe:

Chow Mein

1 pound chopped meat mix-
ture (lung and heart)
1 cup celery
½ cup onion, diced
1 cup bean sprouts
a few pimiento slices
mushrooms (as much as you
can afford)

wheat germ (about 2 heaping
tablespoons)
yeast (whatever you can sneak
in—at least 2 tablespoons)
soy sauce (to taste)
3 cups cooked brown rice

First brown the meat in a heavy pot. Use a little chicken
fat or oil just to start it. Add the vegetables and the bean
sprouts. Add the wheat germ and yeast. If you have some
cooked chicken or other leftover meat, you can add it to
the pot. Don't forget the pimientos for color, and, of course,
the mushrooms. If you have water chestnuts and bamboo
shoots, they will enhance the marvelous mixture of flavors
and texture. Sliced Jerusalem artichokes are a great stand-in
for water chestnuts and very inexpensive. When it is thoroughly heated, throw in a fistful of almonds and ½ cup of
sunflower seeds. Serve this with brown rice and chow mein
noodles. This mixture should be heated—but never over-
cooked. Overcooking kills vitamins and destroys flavors. If
you must reheat it, add more yeast to replace the values
heating destroyed.

When you eat toasted bread, you lose much of its meager
B_1 content. B_1 is destroyed by roasting at high temperatures. When you cook your vegetables, it goes into the
water. Tobacco, alcohol and sugar destroy thiamine in your
body.

If you have a burning and dryness of the eyes;
If your lips chap, if your feet burn;
If you have disorders of the cornea of the eye;
If you have scaliness of the nose, forehead and ears;
If you feel trembly, dizzy or sluggish.

You may need more vitamin B_2 (riboflavin).

Riboflavin is used with B_1 to convert carbohydrates to
energy. It aids your vision, protects hair, nerves, skin, lips
and tongue.

You will get lots of riboflavin in brewer's yeast, liver,
kidney, heart, whey, eggs, soybeans and soy flour, whole
wheat products, hazel nuts, peanuts and hickory nuts. Add
soy powder to gravies, stews, and to ground meat. Use as a

coating instead of bread crumbs. It greatly improves flavor and nutrition.

Be aware that this vitamin is easily destroyed by exposure to light. Milk standing in daylight loses 50 to 70 per cent of its riboflavin in 2 hours. Meat, in see-through containers displayed in the butcher's showcase, loses a goodly portion of its vitamin B_2. Alkaline solutions like baking soda destroy B_2. Try this delicious soya shake for a B_2 pick-up.

Soy Shake

1 tablespoon soy powder	1 cup certified raw milk or
2 tablespoons carob powder	soy milk
a few drops of vanilla	½ cup cracked ice
1 cup water	1 banana, sliced
	1 teaspoon honey

Pour water into mixer or blender, add soy, carob, and vanilla and blend well. Add milk, ice, honey and sliced banana, blend thoroughly. Berries, cherries, peaches or any other fruit may be used instead of banana.

Your deficiencies are showing:
If you are overly anxious;
If you hear voices and there's no one there;
If you are dizzy, irritable, subject to depression;
If you feel numb in various parts of your body;
If you feel as though you are losing your memory;
If your gums are tender;
If you have a swollen, bright red tongue;
If you have no get-up-and-go.

You may have a niacin deficiency (B_3).

Sometimes called the anti-pellagra vitamin, niacin has been used in massive doses to bring schizophrenics back to the world of reality and good health. It promotes healthy liver function, improves poor circulation that keeps your feet cold. It helps digestion. It is helpful in some cases of migraine and disturbed hearing.

You'll find niacin in wheat germ, and wheat bran, brewers yeast, desiccated and fresh liver, beef heart, salmon, prunes, lentils, kidney, chicken, peanut butter and peanuts. One of the best sources is sunflower seeds. For a high-powered niacin dish, try sweet and sour heart. It's delicious.

Sweet and Sour Heart

1 beef heart cut into cubes	½ cup apple cider vinegar
4 tablespoons hot melted shortening (chicken fat if you have it or cold-pressed oil)	4 tablespoons water
	4 tablespoons honey
	2 tablespoons soy flour
1½ cups stewed tomatoes	1 teaspoon sea salt
	paprika

Sauté heart 5 to 10 minutes. Add tomatoes, vinegar, water, honey. Cover and simmer 35 to 40 minutes. Brown flour in hot melted shortening, stir in some gravy. Add to the pot and cook 5 minutes. Add salt and paprika—and enjoy the zesty aroma and flavor.

The more sugar and starch in your diet, the more niacin you need.

Your deficiencies are showing:
If you are pale and wan;
If you have so-called "tired blood";
If you are always "pooped";
If you are getting brownish spots on your face and hands;
If you can hardly climb a flight of stairs without panting.

You may need more folic acid.

The most common deficiency of a water soluble vitamin seen in America today, particularly in pregnancy, is that of folic acid. The local pharmacy cannot supply us with any multiple-vitamin formula containing folic acid. They don't have any. Eat fresh, dark-green uncooked vegetables for more folic acid.

Go creative with your salads, Dr. J. D. Walters of California advises that you taste over 200 different foods in the course of a year—foods grown in different soils as well as different foods. In this way, you are better assured of a supply of all the trace minerals—some of which are depleted in foods that are fertilized with chemicals.

Add lots of different kinds of greens to your salads—beet leaves, chicory, lettuce, spinach, Swiss chard, cucumbers, green peppers, raw string beans, parsley, dill, carrot tops, turnip greens, and some kind of sprout. Sometimes, add olives to your salad for variety and extra nutrition.

Always keep something sprouting on the kitchen sink. Vary the sprout—use fenugreek, wheat, rye, oat, corn, barley, alfalfa seeds, mung beans.

Try this:

Dark Green & Orange Salad

1 bunch leaf lettuce, shredded (use the dark green variety when you can get it)	½ cup sprouts (any kind you may have)
2 cups torn spinach leaves	4 chopped green onions
1 bunch watercress, shredded	12 pitted ripe olives
24 carrot curls	12 raw almonds or cashews

Combine greens, carrot curls, sprouts, and onions. Stuff olives with the nuts. Add to salad. Just before serving, toss with your favorite salad dressing. Serves 6 heavy eaters.

Your deficiencies are showing:
If your skin is dry and rough;
If you have pimples or acne;
If you are susceptible to eye infections;
If you get frequent colds;
If you suspect a malfunction of the genito-urinary system;
If you get frequent infections, like tonsillitis, bronchitis, sinusitis;
If you feel your eyes are tired;
If you are sensitive to bright light;
If you cannot see well at twilight.

You may need more vitamin A.

Many of us are limping through life with inadequate stores of vitamin A and thus robbing the body of its ability to defend itself against infections.

Weightwatchers who have been avoiding fats like the plague are deluding themselves if they think they are getting all the vitamin A they need from the carotene in carrots and other vegetables. Carotene is inefficiently absorbed unless the diet contains a sufficient quantity of oil or fat.

But the greatest villain is the widespread use of commercial high nitrogen fertilizers. They have a devastating effect on vitamin A. Because of these fertilizers, the plant foods eaten by us and by livestock are loaded with nitrates, which make it impossible for our bodies to convert carotene into usable vitamin A.

Remember that the same destructive nitrates are frequently added to packaged food—especially meats, as preservatives. Every time you go to the ball game and feast on hot dogs you are sending a foul ball to your defense system. Sausages, canned meats, cured meats and fish and pickled meats are treated with both sodium nitrite and sodium nitrate. If the kids are hooked on hot dogs, try this recipe. They look like hot dogs and taste better.

Karnatzlach

Children love these. And they have no nitrates!

1½ pounds ground meat mixture	2 eggs slightly beaten
1 grated onion	dash of kelp
1 large grated carrot	¼ teaspoon paprika
1 clove garlic (minced)	¼ cup wheat germ
pinch of thyme, marjoram and oregano or 2 teaspoons poultry seasoning	2 tablespoons yeast

Combine all ingredients except the last 3. Mix well and form into rolls about the diameter of a frankfurter and about 2 to 3 inches long, tapering at each end. Roll in ¼ cup wheat germ, yeast and paprika.

Broil under moderate heat on a slightly oiled rack. Turn to brown on all sides. Serve with hot tomato sauce.

While many of us cannot, because of the nitrates, make the conversion from carotene to vitamin A, everyone can assimilate the vitamin A in fish liver oil which also contains vitamin D. These two vitamins work together, each improving the assimilation of the other.

Don't ever try to sneak fish liver oil into any food concoction. Its flavor and aroma are strong, distinctive and pervasive. You could spoil your creative efforts and turn off the whole family. Also they would get suspicious and look for other evidence of your sneaky strategy. In order to get fish liver oil into the kids, you add it to their morning supplements to be swallowed with fruit juice. If they complain about the increasing number of supplements sitting by their breakfast plates, just tell them casually, "Don't count them—just take them." You'll be surprised how they will.

Your deficiencies are showing:
If you have pink toothbrush;
If you bruise easily and have frequent unexplained black and blue marks;
If you have varicose veins;
If you have a run down feeling;
If your gums are spongy;
If disc lesions give you an aching back.

You very likely need much more vitamin C and vitamin P—the bioflavonoids—than you are getting.

These factors speed the healing of wounds, fight infection and tooth decay, help the liver to fight off the adverse effects of pollution and harmful chemicals, help to build up immunity, prevent hemorrhaging and improve the health of the blood vessels. They help the body to withstand stress conditions and promote the integrity of collagen, which is the connective tissue holding your body cells together. Without sufficient vitamins C and P, your defense structures break down so that you become easy prey to invading organisms. Because collagen is basic to the muscles and bones of the back, vitamin C has been used successfully in the treatment of spinal disc lesions.

Teeth become loose in an individual deficient in this vitamin. This is because the collagen holding them to the gums has deteriorated.

A person who smokes is very likely to be deficient in vitamin C. Smoking destroys, or neutralizes to a large extent, what little vitamin C is taken in food. For instance, one cigarette as ordinarily inhaled, tends to destroy about 25 milligrams of vitamin C or the amount you get in the average orange.

Your requirements for vitamin C vary according to the stresses to which you are subjected. You may need more today than you needed yesterday. While the usual recommended dose of vitamin C is 75 milligrams daily, Dr. Linus Pauling, a Nobel laureate in chemistry, maintains that "daily ingestion of three to six grams (3,000 to 6,000 mg.) of ascorbic acid leads to increased vigor, increased protection against infectious disease, including the common cold, and to an increased rate of healing of wounds." He maintains that a tenfold increase in the daily intake of vitamin C could bring about a 10 percent increase in both physical and mental well being.

Paprika is a good source of vitamin C. Dust it lavishly on salads, cole slaw, potato salad, scrambled eggs, soups. I put a dash of paprika on meat dishes like chow mein or meat balls or hamburgers just before I bring them to the table. It gives food an appetizing glow and adds a touch of piquancy to the flavor.

Use rose hip powder in cold beverages, and take rose hip tablets as a supplement. Use rose hips in tea. Steep for 4 minutes for a beautiful pink drink. If your family favors the traditional orange pekoe, add a handful of rose hips to the tea pot. Other good sources of vitamin C are peppers, oranges, dandelion and turnip greens, watercress, guavas, raspberries, strawberries, kale, kohlrabi, parsley, raw cabbage, broccoli (especially the leaf), grapefruit, blackberries, lemons, spinach, onions and sprouts.

Try some roses on your menu for a tremendous gift to your body and your spirits. Add rose hip powder to applesauce. If you must use canned fruit, pour off the sugar syrup. Make your own syrup using honey, rose hip powder and some unsweetened fruit juice or water.

Do you find yourself reaching for a tranquilizer?

Don't. Take calcium instead. It relaxes the nerves and eases pain. Bone meal is a good source and with dolomite will supply the trace minerals you need to work in partnership with the vitamins, and help you to enjoy abundant good health. Add bone meal powder to cold blender drinks. Carob powder, bone meal, fertile egg and raw milk is our favorite milk shake.

Try this recipe for bone meal cookies. I found it in an unusual cookbook, *Wheat and Sugar Free*, by Mrs. Frieda Nusz, Menno, South Dakota.

Bone Meal Cookies

2 eggs	Pour in bowl, add:
1 cup pitted dates, blended smooth	3 tablespoons carob powder
½ cup oil	1 cup bone meal powder

Bake at 325° until done or set. Cookies will be soft.

I have not covered all the possible deficiency states—only the most common. You have probably noticed that certain foods appear in every vitamin line-up like the recurring theme in a symphony. They are nutritional yeast, wheat germ, wheat germ oil, liver, fish liver oil and rose hips. If your diet and supplements provide you a full complement of these foods, you need not fear a deficiency of any vitamin—very likely not even those that are yet to be discovered.

You might well wonder how come an intelligent, well-educated woman like Mrs. J. didn't have the know-how to apply sensible nutrition to her life so she could enjoy good health and a good figure, too.

It's a reasonable question. Mrs. J., like so many others with a comparable background, prided herself on her intellect. She was fascinated by psychology and was taking a course at the local college. She learned that every child, every husband, every wife and every grandma needs love, affection, appreciation and attention. She was bending her id and ego in an effort to spread these sentiments around like a mantle of snowflakes. Food and nutrition just didn't grab her interest.

She didn't learn that all the lovely intellectual intangibles melt like snowflakes on a hot stove when our bodies are starved for the food elements we must have for a healthy, happy disposition and an optimistic outlook.

She didn't learn that if nerve endings are raw, love won't insulate them. Vitamin B will.

There are many things that nutrition cannot control. That is true. But, let's face it. Whatever breaks or disappointments life throws your way, you're going to be able to field them with a lot more creative energy when you have good nutrition working for you.

Chapter XIV

Change Your Snacks and Save Your Heart

*An adjustment in your nighttime nibbling
can go a long way in helping your heart.*

Has it ever occurred to you that as you sit in front of the TV, and nibble on pretzels, potato chips or jelly beans, you are actually paving the way to a heart attack? Not only are you adding pounds to your hips, which is not good for your silhouette or your ticker, but you are also consuming salt and sugar which research shows upset the chemical balance vital to good heart health.

You can, however, by making some smart substitutions on your snack table, increase your go power, enjoy some delightful new taste sensations, lose weight and add increased endurance to your jogging program—and to your heart.

Let's say, for example, that you have just completed your evening jogging session and your graduated program of calisthenics. You feel great—not only physically but psychologically. You've done your heart a good turn, brought increased oxygen to every cell in your body, and decreased the possibility of your cholesterol ganging up in clots. Fine.

Now you turn on the TV and slump into an easy chair. Why not? You're entitled to a little reward. You're right so far, but watch your next step. You, and probably thousands of others, automatically reach out for one of those snacks that somehow go hand to mouth with watching TV—a highly salted pretzel, potato chip, salted nut or a gum drop. Stop! Salt and sugar are both your enemies when it comes to building cardiovascular health and fitness.

Does this mean that you must keep your hands in your pockets when you watch TV? Not at all. There are delicious snacks that will actually join forces with your jogging program to keep your arteries and heart muscles forever young. Although it may seem impossible to do, pleasant tasting snacks can be made without sugar. Another point to keep in mind is that those snacks should be low in sodium and high in potassium.

Salt, you see, is the enemy of potassium and potassium is your heart's best friend. Research has shown that potassium is vital to the life of the cell, while sodium is an intruder from the surrounding fluid. When potassium is low, it is as if there were a chink in the cell wall and sodium, the enemy lurking at the gate, barges in. Salt then changes the acid-alkaline balance (pH) of the cell, making for a toxic condition which fosters the formation of necrotic (dead) tissue. That dead tissue may block the arteries and is the prelude to sudden death from a heart attack.

But, you may protest, doesn't my body need some salt? Yes, a little. About a gram a day. Most of us consume 10 times that much. There is so much salt in all processed foods, you cannot help getting more than you need.

How does the potassium get into the picture? Recently Dr. P. Prioreschi revealed that there is one particular nutrient which, in almost every case, helps to counteract the effects of the cardiotoxins. That mineral is potassium.

Dr. Prioreschi cited 14 different experiments on animals in which cardiac necroses were induced by various medications and sodium chloride (salt). All of the heart damage or cardiopathies were prevented in the group which got potassium. As a matter of fact, when there is heart trouble ahead, it can be detected before it happens by running a check on the potassium level of the blood.

It is extremely important for athletes, or anyone going in for an extended program of exercise, to insure good potassium stores. Any muscular activity taps our supply of potassium and as potassium goes down in the cell, sodium goes up.

The danger of too much sodium cannot be ignored since modern foods, commercially grown and prepared, seem to have a tastelessness that calls for more and more salt to give them flavor. Considering how much sodium most of us get, and considering that potassium is richest in fruits and vegetables not especially popular among Americans, it is easy to believe that many of us may be walking around with definite potassium shortages.

Can you adjust to life without salt? It's easier than you think. Life without a salt shaker can be plenty spicy. Go creative with all kinds of herbs—dill, oregano, rosemary, thyme, basil, caraway, sesame and poppy seeds—and you will never miss the salt shaker. Have you been putting salt on your eggs? Try chopped chives. Spice up your tomatoes with a little basil. Try rosemary on your lamb, nutmeg on your broccoli. Try roasting meats with onions and a few bay leaves for a truly irresistible aroma and flavor.

At the same time that you cut down on your salt, make an effort to increase your potassium-rich foods. While potassium is present in many foods and you would probably think a deficiency would be unlikely, such is not the case. A large amount of potassium in foods, for example, is bound with protein when subjected to the heat of cooking, making it less available.

A diet containing liberal quantities of raw fruits and vegetables may provide an adequate dietary intake of potassium with limited amounts of sodium—both desirable objectives. Other excellent sources of potassium are bran, corn, eggs, fish, legumes, liver, nuts, oatmeal, bone meal, prunes (especially raw), raisins, whole grains, grapes, yeast, onions, tomatoes, strawberries, and especially seeds, seeds, seeds.

Why not fill your snack dishes with seeds? Throw in a few raw cashews, almonds, peanuts and raisins and you'll have a tempting snack you can munch to your heart's content and for your heart's content.

Preparing other healthful and taste tempting snacks is quite simple. Here are two simple recipes:

Carob Confection

Blend together:

½ cup carob powder
½ cup honey
½ cup peanut butter (natural —not hydrogenated)

½ cup sunflower seeds
½ cup sesame seeds
¼ cup wheat germ
¼ cup soya grits or soy flour

Mix together. Form into balls. Roll in coconut crumbs (unsweetened). This makes a delicious healthful snack, rich in vitamins, minerals, low in sodium and high in potassium. Natural peanut butter and coconut merge with the flavor of carob to form an irresistible treat.

Pineapple Porcupines

1 pineapple
1 cup honey

1 cup wheat germ, sunflower or sesame seeds

Remove eyes of peeled pineapple with paring knife and cut pineapple into pieces approximately two inches square. Insert toothpick into each square to act as a handle. Now dip the cubes into the honey, then roll them in the wheat germ, sesame seeds or sunflower seeds. You may put them on a tray in the freezer to harden until snack time or serve all ingredients on your cocktail table as a "do-it-yourself" dip. This one is especially refreshing in warm weather.

Chapter XV

Have a Healthy Party and Make It a Smash!

Even those who watch the kind of food they eat 52 weeks out of the year, often let their guard down when it comes to giving a party.

The health-conscious party-giver reasons: "It's only once. Besides I owe it to my friends to serve the kind of things they like and are used to."

But throwing a healthful party is no more involved than having the ordinary kind—and it can be a real smash. The ordinary hors d'oeuvres served at the run-of-the-mill party are hardly conversation starters. But they will be at a healthful party. Everyone likes new experiences, and the new and delicious foods you can treat your guests to will be a thoughtful way for you to say "Enjoy yourself."

Your right-hand man in party planning is the manager of your local health food or specialty foods store. He will probably have in stock the ingredients of all the recipes you will be using. And he will have a wide variety of other foods that we will not discuss here but which you may wish to add to your list.

Tidbits

Honey-coated pumpkin seeds will be a big hit with your guests. They taste a bit like candy-coated peanuts. To make them yourself is unnecessarily time consuming. You can buy them at most health food stores. Also, pick up some carob bars. Carob has a flavor similar to chocolate, but is more creamy and milder. Other candies, sweetened with honey, are also available.

Perhaps you would like to make your own candies, too. Here are four recipes for you to consider:

Sunflower Seed Candies

Blend 2 cups of sunflower seeds to a fine meal. Start with the blender cover on and then remove cover and push seeds down with a spatula. Always do this carefully, keeping far away from the cutting blade. Add 1 heaping tablespoon of honey to one cup of the ground seeds; 1 heaping tablespoon of peanut butter and a dash of vanilla to the other cup. Stir into dough, form into balls or desired shapes and roll in coating mixtures.

Sesame Seed Candies

In blender:
2 cups sesame seeds   ½ cup oil

Start blender with cover on and run it awhile. Take the cover off and help push seeds down and under. Add 2 tablespoons honey and a dash of vanilla to running blender. Blend until smooth. Divide into three bowls. Add 1 tablespoon peanut butter to one, 1 tablespoon carob to the second. Leave one plain. Shape into balls. Do not coat these. They resemble fudge.

Sesame Taffy

In blender:
1 cup sesame seeds   vanilla and a bit of almond
½ cup oil   flavoring
enough honey to sweeten, if
    desired

Start blender and keep seeds turning down and under with rubber scraper. Let it run a long time until mixture gets hot and looks glossy. Turn out into bowl. With rubber scraper knead up on side of bowl, squeezing out the oil. Finish kneading with your hands, squeezing out the oil. Roll this dough into a log and slice.

Pumpkin Seed Candy

In blender:

2 cups pumpkin seeds	½ cup of oil from sesame taffy
2 tablespoons honey	dash of pure vanilla

Drop by teaspoons into coating mixtures. Chill.

A heaping tablespoon of honey in these recipes means swirling the spoon until you can lift it to the bowl without dripping. This actually is more than a level tablespoon.

Freeze all of these separately on a cookie sheet. Then throw them into freezer containers to store in the freezer.

Unsalted seeds and nuts are always popular. Roasted sunflower seeds are delicious. As a special touch, dip the roasted seeds in water, shake off excess moisture, put them in a sack with onion powder and shake well.

An old Hebrew custom which will fit in perfectly is to slice apples in quarter-inch sections and place them in a ring around a small bowl of honey. Dipping the apple in the honey and eating it conveys the wish for a sweet and fruitful year.

Cold meat tidbits on tooth picks are good dipping. It will surprise you how you can glamorize parts of cooked chicken, turkey, goose, duck, even giblet bits, or roast beef bits by serving them on a toothpick. These could be served with a corn muffin or corn bread slices too, on which a honey and peanut butter mixture has been spread.

A liver paste spread on rye crackers is not only rich in flavor—but also in the B vitamins. Here is a recipe you may want to use:

Chopped Liver

Broil one pound of chicken livers, sauté one chopped onion in oil or chicken fat. Hard boil two eggs. Reserve one egg yolk for garnish.

Chop all ingredients together in a wooden bowl with two or three lettuce leaves and a little parsley. If you like a finer texture, you may put all ingredients into the blender. Garnish with egg yolk strained through a sieve.

From your specialty foods store you will also be able to buy a large variety of jams and butters. Sesame butter makes a tasty spread, but has a taste which will be foreign to the non-health-food-oriented palate. If your guests fit into this category, better stick with cashew and almond butter and the preserves to which no sugar has been added.

Crackers for your spread which are free of all undesirable ingredients are difficult to come by, even in health food stores. The simplest approach is to choose one of the following recipes and make your own. Mixing them will not take more than a few minutes, and in quantity they will be less expensive than if you were to purchase them anyway.

Cornmeal Crackers

1 cup yellow cornmeal
½ teaspoon sea salt
1 tablespoon soy oil

⅞ cup boiling water
¼ cup sesame seeds

Combine ingredients; drop by tablespoons on oiled baking sheet; spread in 3 or 4 inch rounds. Bake at 400 degrees until golden. Poppy or other seeds may be substituted for the sesame seeds.

Canapé Crackers

(Good with soup or jam too)

1½ cups soy flour
1½ cups corn flour
¼ cup soy or corn oil

½ cup water (least bit less than ½)
2 eggs

Sift flour into mixing bowl. Make a well in center and pour in oil, water and beaten eggs. Stir until it forms a ball of dough. (Should be slightly moist, not dry. If necessary, add a bit of water.) Pinch off pieces and shape into 1-inch balls; set on greased or oiled cookie sheet and flatten. Bake at 325 degrees for 10-12 minutes.

Corn Crisp Crackers

1 cup stone ground cornmeal
1 tablespoon oil

½ teaspoon kelp
⅞ cup boiling water

Combine all ingredients; make balls using one tablespoon mixture for each. Place on oiled baking sheet, and pat or mash into three-inch rounds. Bake in hot oven (400 degrees) for 30 minutes. Makes 2 dozen.

Oatmeal Crackers

Here is a health cracker to nibble on that is surprisingly tasty.

Blend together:

1 cup potato water	1 teaspoon sea kelp
½ cup cooking oil	4 cups quick-cooking oatmeal

(You can use the old-fashioned rolled oats and whiz it up fairly fine, a cup at a time, in the blender, if you wish.) Mix the ingredients into a stiff dough and chill it in the refrigerator. Lightly flour a board and roll the dough very thin. Sprinkle with caraway seeds and roll these in. Now transfer the thin pastry to an oiled cookie sheet. Cut in squares and prick with fork tines. Bake at 350 degrees about 20 minutes.

To add to the holiday atmosphere, a bowl or two of fruit is essential. Sprigs of fresh mint could line the bowl and contrast with the brightly colored fruit.

Treats

Anyone who thinks healthful eating is dull eating will have a change of heart after these amazing dishes:

Coconut Banana Meringue Pie

4 eggs	4 bananas
⅓ cup date sugar	1½ cups flaked, unsweetened
1½ cups crushed almonds	coconut
2 tablespoons almond butter	1 teaspoon lemon juice

Blend almond butter with crushed almonds. Then press into a pie plate and refrigerate. Mash bananas with a fork. Stir in lemon juice, then coconut. Pour into crust after crust has been refrigerated half an hour. Separate yolks from whites of eggs and beat whites into meringue, adding the date sugar. Cover pie with meringue mixture. Keep refrigerated until just before serving. This treat will be especially appreciated by those of your guests who have a sweet tooth. But you can rest assured that all the sweetness is from natural sources—dates, bananas and almonds.

Peach Rice Betty

1 cup brown rice (3 cups when cooked)	juice of one lemon
	½ cup honey
3 or 4 good-sized peaches	½ cup chopped walnuts
sprinkle of unsweetened coconut	

Oil a glass baking dish. Spread a layer of brown rice, then a layer of thinly sliced peaches mixed with nuts and lemon juice; another layer of rice, then peach mixture. Dribble with the honey and top with coconut. Bake at 350 degrees for 30 minutes or until peaches are soft.

Ambrosia Cream

1 pint sour cream or 1 pint yogurt
crushed pineapple—unsweetened

½ cup walnuts
½ cup coconut—unsweetened
1 pound of seedless grapes
2 oranges

Drain pineapple. Peel and section oranges. Mix all ingredients together. Garnish with a few orange sections. Add a little honey, or any good natural jam sweetened with honey, if you need a little more sweetness. Let flavors meld in refrigerator for a few hours before serving.

Beverages

There is no end to the beverages you will be able to serve at your healthful party. Your health food store is well stocked with exotic teas from all over the world. Both fennel and licorice teas are especially appropriate at the holiday season, and you may want to have them available for your guests to sample. But some people, who are not accustomed to new flavor sensations, may not like these two, so be sure to have a good choice of other beverages available.

Two kinds of punch can add special zest to your get-together:

Papaya Punch

6 cups plain soda
2 cups unsweetened cranberry juice
2 cups unsweetened pineapple juice

2 cups camomile tea (This can be bought in tea bags at your health food store.)

After steeping the tea for about five minutes, pour into punch bowl and add other juices. Refrigerate. The camomile not only provides a mellowness to the punch, but also imparts a rich aroma.

Apple-Pineapple Punch

Ahead of time, in a juicer which makes clear fruit juice, put 12 or 14 cored apples, 2 cups raw cranberries and 1 can unsweetened crushed pineapple. Strain this juice into a gallon glass jar and keep at room temperature, and tightly closed.

Also ahead of time, simmer several sticks of cinnamon and a dozen or so cloves in a quart of water. Strain and keep it handy to heat.

When serving time is near, heat the spice water hot, add honey as desired, a cup at least, stir until honey is dissolved and add to the fruit juice. Serve the punch warm or hot, as desired.

As an added touch for cold punch, freeze home-canned strawberries or raspberries in some small ice cube trays and grapes in the others. Add the juice to the trays to make brightly colored cubes. Put into the punch just before serving.

Liver Patties

Liver gets a "pick me up" nibble status and goes to a party.

These patties have lots of the vitamin B's.

1 pound beef or steer liver	Put through meat grinder or
1 medium onion	chop fine in wooden bowl.
½ medium green pepper	Now add a little sea salt
small clove of garlic	¼ cup wheat germ
	1 egg

Mix well and drop by teaspoonful into pan in which 1 tablespoon of corn oil has been heated. Brown well on both sides. They are great hot hors d'oeuvres.

Cooking for a Crowd? Try this Chicken Pilaf

This recipe feeds 30

4 stewing chickens	⅔ tablespoon ground black
¾ gallon chicken stock	pepper
(from cooking chicken)	1 tablespoon minced garlic
½ tablespoon oregano	2 cups chopped onion
½ tablespoon rosemary	4⅔ cups brown rice
½ tablespoon sweet basil	

Fry: 1 cup slivered almonds in oil
Brown: 3 cups monukka raisins in oil

Sauté onions and garlic in oil. Stir raw rice into this. Add seasonings. Add stock. Cook for one hour total. Add pre-cooked chicken, and raisins. Top with almonds.

How to Make Dry-Roasted Soy Nuts

Soak soy beans overnight. Rinse. Boil for about an hour in fresh water to which a little sea salt has been added. Drain. Now spread the beans on an oiled cookie sheet and roast in 350 degree oven for about an hour or until brown. Sprinkle with kelp while they are still warm. Serve to delighted guests.

Great for dips

Corn Chips

2 cups cornmeal   ½ teaspoon sea salt
3 tablespoons raw peanut flour   1½ cups boiling water
4 tablespoons corn oil

Put cornmeal in mixing bowl. Add three heaping tablespoons of raw peanut flour and sea salt. Mix dry ingredients, then add about one and one-half cups of boiling water, gradually. Dough should be moist but not sticky. Add corn oil and mix thoroughly. Cover bowl and allow mixture to cool for about an hour. Form into patties and lay on oiled cookie sheet. Bake in 375 degree oven until edges are brown, about 45 to 50 minutes. These make ideal snacks and can be used as a bread substitute.

Chapter XVI

How to Lose Weight—
And Feel Great—
Without Hardly Dieting

If you have been practicing sneaky cookery for more than a month, you have increased your go-power and, if you were overweight, you have slimmed down without even trying. In fact, you never suffered a hunger pang or a conscience pang. You never indulged in a cookie binge, not because you were counting calories, but because you just had no desire for sweets. You've been getting all the sweets you need from the fresh fruit you've been serving for dessert. And from the fruit, the enzymes that help digest the protein you eat. Because this converts your food into energy more efficiently, you are experiencing more vitality. You've been moving about with more zip, more poise and more grace. This is the kind of movement which burns up excess calories. ˋ

If you have hit a plateau and would like to lose a little more weight, observe these suggestions:

1. Never eat what the kids leave over—just because it is a shame to throw it out. If you just can't stand this kind of waste, get a dog, feed the birds, or start a compost pile.

2. Never eat anything standing up. You'd be surprised how many calories you consume just tasting as you prepare dinner. If you must keep your jaws going, do it on fresh, raw vegetables. Always keep some available in the refrigerator.

3. Always eat a good, high protein breakfast.

4. Go to bed early before you get snack happy. Better to go to bed with a light stomach and wake up with a ravenous appetite. Then you'll enjoy that big high-protein breakfast. What you eat in the morning gives you much more go-power, calorie for calorie. In other words, if you consume the same amount of calories as your friend, but get more of yours at breakfast, while she gets more of hers at night, you will burn up more calories than your friend, and you will lose weight faster.

5. Never eat an empty calorie and you'll never need to count calories. That means nothing made with sugar or refined flour. That means no sugar buns, no doughnuts, no macaroni or spaghettti or things of that nature, and, of course, no sugar.

What shall I have for dessert? When all around you are indulging in apple pie or cheese cake, be bold. Ask for an apple, or a pear or a piece of melon in season. Any restaurant worth returning to will serve you a bowl of fruit for dessert, if you request it. This kind of meal topper will leave you with a fresh taste in your mouth; it will clean your teeth and it will give you valuable vitamins and minerals with not an empty calorie in a bite.

6. If you've been skipping meals in order to lose weight —*don't!* When a meal is missed, so much stored fat pours into the bloodstream that the fat content of the blood often rises to 6 times above the normal. This can be dangerous for the heart. Furthermore, all of us are carrying excessive amounts of DDT in our bodies, and this DDT is stored in our body fat. As the fat melts, the DDT gets into the bloodstream and could cause a toxic condition. Of course, you want to melt body fat, but do it slowly and make sure you get plenty of the C and B vitamins. They work to detoxify

the poisons in your body fat, along with their numerous other benefits.

7. Never eat to get full. As soon as the edge is off your appetite and you're comfortable, don't take another bite. Tell yourself "Ten seconds on the lips—ten years on the hips." This may be difficult to do for a day or two. Then your stomach will be flatter and you will have a reduced capacity. It will take less food to satisfy your appetite.

8. Try reversing your meals to lose weight. Dr. Harvey Smith, a specialist in treating overweight, believes that 90 per cent of American fatties could lose weight by merely reversing the order of their daily meals: eat breakfast at dinner time and dinner in the morning.

The theory makes a lot of sense. The calories for meals eaten early in the day are burned off by the day's activities. Calories consumed in the evening at dinner time have less chance to be consumed and frequently turn into fat. Dr. Smith believes that eating habits should be rearranged so that as many as 80 per cent of the day's calories are contained in breakfast and lunch, leaving just 20 per cent for dinner time. This is one way a weight-watcher can enjoy all the calories his body needs, suffer no hunger pangs, and trim his figure at the same time.

9. Eat fat and lose weight. If you have been on one of the current austere weight reducing programs, you will probably do a double take at this caption. But, we're not kidding. There is much evidence that fat in your diet does not mean fat on your hips. Quite the contrary. According to Ray N. Lawson, M.D., who shed 35 pounds in one year, you can eat fat and grow slim. What's more, you will enjoy a much happier disposition, feel pleasantly satisfied and you'll be able to partake of many of the delectable foods you have been denying yourself.

Only a few years ago, doctors were advising "no fat" diets for the overweight. In fact, many medical eyebrows still twitch at the suggestion of fat for the obese. But day by day, doctors are beginning to be aware of the downright danger of omitting fats from the diet. For one thing, vitamin A, being fat-soluble and always closely associated with animal fat, is either poorly absorbed or cannot be absorbed at all, without fats. Therefore, a diet low in fat means low vitamin A utility.

Besides, doctors are finding out that eating fat does not add weight and, in fact, a diet high in fats and proteins and low (very low) in carbohydrates is the speediest, healthiest, and, indeed, the happiest way to shed pounds. Remember that eating fats acts on the metabolism of the body for better combustion, or burning up, of the food you do eat. It speeds up the process. In *Eat Fat and Grow Slim* (Collins of Canada), Doctor Richard Macharness of London writes about detailed medical experiments with 3 different diets, of equal caloric value, in which the high fat diet removed excess weight fastest. Don't go overboard on fats because you don't want to lose too fast. Use polyunsaturated oils in cooking and on salads.

10. Do you regularly lose and regain hundreds of pounds by the rhythm method of girth control? You may be one of the countless people who suffer with reactive hypoglycemia, a particular metabolic disorder which can frustrate your best efforts to reduce. At the same time it makes you desperate for the sweets which are forcing your weight up!

Take frequent meals—5 or 6 small ones—instead of three large ones. By eating often, you eat less each time, so that instead of having 3 upward and downward wide swings in blood sugar levels, you will have 6 or 7 small ones. In time, the level tends to smooth out. Small meals are better utilized by the body. They minimize conversion of food into fat and frequent meals cut the tendency to nibble.

11. Be sure to include some lecithin in your diet. Lecithin helps you to feel well-fed on less food. It helps the symmetry of a figure that is heavy in spots. It helps circumvent many of the health problems associated with dieting, like cholesterol deposits and gall bladder complications. There is evidence that it increases your brain power, your stamina and virility while decreasing your girth.

How does it work? The lecithin invades the artery walls and depletes them of fatty plaques which are then deposited in the bloodstream. Once in the bloodstream, the fat is apparently metabolized or burned out. At first, lecithin appears to work in reverse because it raises the fat level in the blood. This is only because it is pulling fat deposits out of other parts of the body—from those stubborn fat areas you so often have wished would melt away.

12. Avoid coffee. Anyone trying to lose weight who drinks black coffee to still the pangs of hunger is only making matters worse. The repeated stimulus to the insulin producing organs in the pancreas makes them more sensitive and the resultant low blood sugar only makes a rigid diet harder to live with. Dieting to reduce is much easier if coffee, and caffeine in other forms, such as strong tea, chocolate and soft drinks are excluded.

13. Don't—don't—substitute artificially sweetened foods for the sugared variety. The idea, after all, is to retrain your tastebuds so that you no longer experience a craving for sweets. Secondly, you want to build good health. Artificial sweeteners of all kinds are highly suspect.

14. Start an exercise program—preferably outdoors. While exercise encourages appetite, it does not encourage excessive food consumption. With exercise, you eat less but enjoy it more.

Stay with this regimen and you will not only lose excess weight, you will feel great. Losses exceeding a hundred pounds have been achieved on this program—and not with starvation. The cravings for foods high in starch and sugar tend to disappear permanently. In fact, these foods actually become distasteful to you.

The ultimate rewards? Clearer, more beautiful skin, more energy, an increased ability to cope, more days bursting with health, vigor and the joy of living, and a figure that looks great in a bathing suit.

Must I Count Calories? No. The rule is Never Eat an Empty Calorie and You'll Never Have to Count the Calories. All the rest is common sense.

Here's a great recipe that's full of nutrients. Try it for a good hearty breakfast that sticks to your ribs; it's also great for lunch or dinner and one that you can serve to guests with pride.

Oriental Rice

Sauté a half cup finely chopped onion in two tablespoons soy oil. When the onion is limp and golden, add one cup of cooked brown rice. Stir. Add finely chopped leftover chicken, beef or tuna fish. Now add a half cup of finely chopped celery, a half cup of drained bean sprouts. Mix some more. Break an egg into the pan and mix the ingredients all together until the egg is all through the dish. Dust with finely chopped fresh parsley. Season to taste with freshly grated ginger root, curry powder, red pepper, and sea salt or kelp. Remove to hot platter. Now garnish with slivered almonds and grated coconut. Man, that's good eating. This serves one hearty eater.

Here's another good recipe to lose weight by. They're called "French Fries" because that's what they look like. But they're different because they have practically no calories even though they are crisp and delicious.

Take a can of Italian green beans and drain them. Place the beans on a cookie sheet; sprinkle with ¼ teaspoon sea salt or kelp. Bake in a hot oven (400 degrees) for 10 minutes or until beans are brown and crisp. Remove from oven and enjoy. This is enough for an intimate duo.

Try out this French toasted cheese sandwich for raves.

For each portion use one slice whole wheat bread, one ounce of a good cheese, preferably one that is unprocessed, one egg and a half teaspoon sea salt.

Use a sharp knife and cut through the bread horizontally. You may find it easier to do this if the bread is lightly toasted first. Place cheese between the bread slices. Beat up egg and salt in a flat bottomed soup bowl. Dip all sides of each sandwich in the egg mixture. Place in pre-heated skillet or in a 350° oven in a glass baking dish. Cook until well browned on both sides. Serve with satisfaction.

Carrot Nut Torte

This is a delicious low calorie cake. It has no shortening, no baking powder and no baking soda. Carrots give it vitamin A. Walnuts and eggs give it protein and B vitamins.

1 cup grated carrots	½ cup honey plus
1 cup walnuts	2 tablespoons
1 cup hi-protein flour (whole wheat, soy, rice and wheat germ)	1 teaspoon cinnamon
	6 eggs

Separate eggs. Beat yolks and honey until light and creamy. Add grated carrots, coarsely broken nuts, flour and cinnamon. Beat whites until stiff. Fold into mix. Pour into 8 × 8-inch glass cake dish. Bake in 350 degree oven 45 minutes.

You can use this batter to make cup cakes. Put a few in the children's lunch boxes. They sure beat store-bought cookies for the food elements that build sturdy bodies.

Baked Jerusalem Artichoke Hash

Put the vegetables for this hash through the food grinder or in the blender with small amounts of water and grind or whiz them fine, adding more until the amounts are obtained.

1 cup raw carrot pulp	½ teaspoon mace
3 cups artichoke pulp	½ teaspoon chili powder
½ cup onion pulp	1 tablespoon sea kelp
1 pound ground beef mixture	

Blend ingredients and pack in an oiled 2-quart casserole dish or in bread tins. Bake until it is done in the center, about 1 hour.

Jerusalem Artichoke Flip

Put scrubbed artichokes through a juicer which makes clear juice for this drink. It doesn't need any flavoring whatever, but you may add herbs or parsley (snipped up fine) on top of the glass for adornment. Drink immediately.

Broiled Chicken and Jerusalem Artichokes

Several hours before preparing, put cooking oil in a bowl with fresh or dried herbs, especially thyme and marjoram. 30 minutes before the chicken is done, slice the scrubbed artichokes and dunk them in the herbed oil and place on a cookie sheet. Place up close to the broiler and brown, remove and turn, and dust with sea kelp. Now brown the other sides, then lay them on the rack around the chicken for slowly cooking through. Serve them on the platter with the chicken arranged around it and garnished with parsley.

Artichoke Salad

Put the following through the food chopper:

2 cups scrubbed artichokes, cubed
1 onion
2 sprigs parsley
½ cup pignolias (pine nuts)

Grind everything into a refrigerator dish and cover. Serve at once. Dressing may be added if desired. Serves 3 or 4.

Desserts
Hi-Pro-Lo-Calorie Frozen Peach Whip

When peaches are plentiful, try to get some that have not been sprayed—even if they aren't so pretty as the commercial variety. It's easier to cut out the brown spots than to remove insecticide residues . . .

1 cup water
½ cup dry milk powder
1 teaspoon vanilla
2 tablespoons yogurt
3 peaches (scrubbed and cut)
2 teaspoons honey or raw sugar for non-weight watchers

Everything goes into the blender till frothy. Pour into paper cups and freeze. Delightful dessert or t.v. snack for a hot night. Hardly any calories—loads of protein, calcium and go-power.

Chicken-Pecan Spread

Serve this delicious spread at your next party—with turnip slices, cucumber slices or stuffed in celery sticks—and your weight-watching friends will love you.

2 cups cooked minced chicken or turkey
¼ cup finely chopped celery
1 pimiento, finely chopped
½ cup chopped pecans
1 tablespoon fresh lime juice
homemade mayonnaise

Combine all ingredients and add enough mayonnaise to suit individual taste. Place mixture in a pretty glass bowl and sprinkle liberally with parsley flakes.

Egg Foo Yung

Squash is a good source of vitamin A. Its low calorie status makes it especially appealing to weight-watchers. This is a good supper dish—with fresh fruit and a tossed salad.

4 medium unpeeled zucchini squash (grated)
1 onion (grated)
3 beaten eggs
1 teaspoon sea salt
½ cup wheat germ

Mix together. Drop by tablespoon on heated griddle or bake on a cookie sheet in 350° oven until nicely browned. Serves 4 nicely.

Almost Raw Pumpkin

A tasty side dish—rich in vitamin A—low in calories, tastes cooked but retains many raw-vegetable enzymes.

2 cups grated raw pumpkin
1½ tablespoons safflower oil
1 teaspoon raw honey (or more)
sea salt and paprika to taste

Combine pumpkin, oil and honey in top of double boiler, cover and cook over boiling water until thoroughly heated. Season with sea salt and paprika and serve piping hot. Serves 3 or 4.

Fresh Cantaloupe Shake

A refreshing beverage—high in flavor—low in calories.

½ cup unsweetened pineapple juice
2 cups sliced or cubed cantaloupe (ripe)

Put juice into blender to start, drop sliced or cubed cantaloupe into blender a few pieces at a time, blending thoroughly. Add more cantaloupe if you desire a thicker shake.

Wonderful for people who are always hungry. It sure fills you up and you don't feel like eating anything else after a glassful. It is wonderful too, to satisfy a child's sweet tooth. If you have any left over, freeze it and serve later as a tasty ice.

Chapter XVII

Who's Afraid of a Sneaky Cook?

Shortly after our four children came home from their annual dental inspection with big no-cavity grins, my husband, deep in an income tax frenzy, announced that we didn't have a single doctor bill to declare an honest deduction.

He was amazed. I was triumphant but I didn't let on. I knew my sneaky cooking was paying dividends.

But, just as you wonder when and how to tell the kids about the birds and the bees, you wonder when and how to let them in on your secret strategy so they will continue to eat in good health even when they have left your tender trap.

But one day I found, amongst the papers left over from homework on the kitchen table, a composition my son had written for an English assignment and I realized that all that good nutrition made them so smart I couldn't fool them no matter how I tried. The name of the composition was:

My Mother Is a Sneaky Cook

Come to dinner at our house. I guarantee that you will be healthier when you leave than you were when you came, but you will never know it. My mother specializes in making people healthy when they are not looking. How she does it is a well-kept secret, but in the past five years of sleuthing, I have been able to uncover a small portion of her strategy.

Take a common, ordinary, everyday food like hamburger. Hamburger is a nutrition food just the way it is, but my mother makes it more so. One day I happened to pick up the upstairs telephone extension and I heard a strange conversation.

"The hamburger-mixture, Mrs. Kinderlehrer, you want it like always?"

"Yes, two pounds of hamburger and one pound each of you-know-what."

"Two pounds of hamburger," the male voice said as if he were writing it down, "one pound heart and one pound lung. Right? You want it in four packages?"

"You'd better put it in three packages. One of the kids always manages to bring a friend when we're having hamburgers."

"No wonder. At home they don't get it so juicy. I'll tell you a little secret, Mrs. Kinderlehrer. When I make up your mixture, I make some extra for my wife. My kids like it too."

"Do they know what's in it?"

"They never asked so I never told them. Do you want maybe a brain this week?"

"Let's see—a brain. You'd better let the brain go till next week. I'm not making anything I can hide it in."

The next episode my brother related to me. One afternoon after school he stumbled into the kitchen to find my mother tending her pots, as usual. Intent on doing homework, my brother was not aware of what my mother was doing until the whir of the blender diverted his attention.

My brother looked at the blender and saw a bowlful of wheat germ. This was no ordinary wheat germ—it was finely ground. It looked like white sugar turned brown. He watched, fascinated, as my mother put more wheat germ in the blender and produced more of the finely-ground grain.

Curious, my brother asked my mother why she was grinding the wheat germ. She replied that she was going to bake a cake for guests who were coming for supper and "it is better that they don't know how healthy they are getting."

Once I watched my mother bake a cake. She started with a mix, but I am still not sure what she ended up with. Where the mix called for sugar, Mom put in half the amount called for—and she used raw sugar. ("White sugar has all the good things taken out of it before it gets to you. At least raw sugar isn't that bad.") She added food yeast ("It's chock full of vitamins and minerals.") and seeds of all different kinds: sesame, sunflower, and pumpkin ("If they're good enough for the birds they're good enough for us!"). The funny thing about it is the cake was delicious.

When you dine at our house, you will probably notice some other things. We never have white rice; we have a mandarin orange and brown rice concoction. Yogurt replaces sour cream, and honey understudies sugar. If guests demand sugar, my mother hands them raw sugar with a sign on the bowl: "Caution, may be hazardous to your health!"

My mother is four feet eleven inches tall, weighs ninety-two pounds, and has more energy than any teenager I know. She maintains that you cannot get fat on good food. You get sturdy, slim, svelte, and sexy—in that order.

Preface to Recipes

Some of the recipes for the good healthy gourmet dishes included in this collection were suggested by readers of *Prevention* and have appeared in the Table Talk section of that magazine.

Poultry, A Nutritional Bonanza

Poultry is very high quality protein. In nutrition studies done at Cornell University, it was shown that the protein content of turkey amounted to 22 percent of the total edible portion in the broadbreasted varieties. In the roasted meat, protein increased as moisture decreased, thus, cooked edible meat of a broiler was 51 percent protein. A large turkey is 56.7 percent protein, ducks 38.4 percent and geese 41.4 percent protein, according to this study. The breast meat of roasted turkeys ranked higher in protein than any of the cooked meats. It is also one of the lowest in fat of all meats and is unusually rich in riboflavin and niacin. Poultry is high in essential fatty acids and relatively low in calories. Like other meats, it furnishes both phosphorus and iron. Turkeys, up to 16 pounds, should be roasted at 325°; larger turkeys are better when they are roasted in a 300° oven.

Sweet and Sour Chicken

¼ cup rice flour
¾ teaspoon sea salt
¼ teaspoon paprika
⅛ teaspoon thyme
1 chicken, disjointed
3 tablespoons salad oil

½ cup chopped onions
¼ cup apple juice or cider
2 tomatoes, peeled and diced
1 tablespoon wine vinegar
1 teaspoon honey
1 tablespoon chopped parsley

Mix the flour, sea salt, paprika and thyme together. Roll the chicken in it until coated.

Heat the oil in a skillet and sauté the chicken and onions until browned on all sides. Add the apple juice, tomato, vinegar and honey. Cover and cook over low heat 25 minutes, or until chicken is tender. Sprinkle with parsley and serve.

Chicken Hawaiian

This is a great meal for a busy Monday—gives you a chance to use up the chicken left over from the weekend—you should be so lucky. You'll need a half cup of orange juice, ¼ cup of barbecue sauce, 2 tablespoons of oil, cut up chicken—about 2 cups, and add a can of pineapple tidbits (unsweetened). Add the juice, too—about 3 tablespoons. It will be a little thin, so add a heaping tablespoon of food yeast—this when they're not looking. Just heat the whole concoction nicely—don't boil. Now throw in a few whole almonds or cashews—or pumpkin seeds.

This dish has such a fragrance! You won't have to call them into dinner. The aroma does. Serve it with satisfaction on top of hot brown rice. Be prepared to serve seconds.

Chicken and Almond Salad

8 slices cooked chicken breast
1 cup celery, chopped
½ cup almonds (slivered)
1 lettuce (Boston)
mayonnaise
1 cup pre-soaked raisins

Dice chicken. Mix with raisins, almonds and celery. Arrange on the lettuce, cover with mayonnaise. Serve chilled.

Chinese Chicken Salad

1 cup cooked chicken
½ cup bamboo shoots, slivered
1 cup coarsely shredded lettuce or Chinese cabbage
1 radish (large), thinly sliced
¼ cup coarsely chopped walnuts
1 cup bean sprouts
3 tablespoons oil
1 tablespoon vinegar
1½ teaspoons soy sauce
¼ teaspoon powdered ginger

Cut the chicken into match-like strips and marinate 20 minutes in soy sauce. In a bowl combine the chicken, bamboo shoots, lettuce, radishes, bean sprouts and nuts. Toss lightly. Mix together the oil, vinegar, soy sauce and ginger until well blended. Pour over the salad, tossing lightly to coat the mixture. Serves 4.

Crunchy Baked Chicken

½ cup safflower oil
1 teaspoon sea salt
1 clove garlic, crushed
½ cup wheat germ
½ teaspoon paprika
2 broilers—about 3 pounds each, cut into serving pieces

In a bowl, combine oil, sea salt, garlic and paprika. Brush chicken pieces with this mixture. Roll each piece in wheat germ. Place, skin side down, in a shallow baking pan and brush each piece again with the oil mixture. Bake in a 350° oven until brown, turn each piece and bake until brown and tender. Serves 4 to 6.

Garden of Eden Casserole

1 3-pound chicken, cut into
serving pieces
1 teaspoon sea salt
½ cup safflower oil

2 large apples, sliced
2 teaspoons honey
¼ cup apple cider

Heat the oil in a large skillet. Sprinkle chicken with seasoning and brown in the hot oil on all sides. Transfer to a baking casserole. Place apple slices between chicken pieces, drizzle with honey and pour cider over all. Cover casserole and bake in a 350 degree oven for about 50 minutes or until chicken is tender. Serve hot to 2 or 3.

Sparkling Chicken Salad

A lovely, make-ahead main dish for a special occasion, buffet, luncheon or a festive family dinner.

2½ cups cold chicken, diced
1 cup white grapes
½ cup shredded almonds
2 tablespoons minced parsley
½ cup chicken stock

1 cup celery, chopped fine
1 teaspoon sea salt
1¼ tablespoons gelatin
4 tablespoons water
1 cup homemade mayonnaise

Mix chicken, celery, grapes, almonds, parsley, and season with sea salt. Soak gelatin in cold water 5 minutes; then dissolve in boiling stock. Add gelatin and chicken stock to mayonnaise and stir until mixture begins to thicken. Fold in chicken mixture. Pack in molds. If desired, place sliced hard-cooked eggs in the bottom of the molds.

Meat Recipes

Soybean Chili

1½ pounds ground beef
¼ cup chopped onion
4 cups cooked soybeans

3 cups tomato puree
1½ cups water (beans cooked in)

Cook meat and onions together, drain off any fat that comes from meat. Then add tomato puree and water; slowly simmer for 30 to 45 minutes. Add the cooked soybeans and heat thoroughly. Serves 4 hearty eaters. Freeze any leftover for a quick meal at later date.

Blender Meat Loaf

1 pound ground beef
¼ cup soaked soybeans
¼ cup cooked brown rice
¼ cup oatmeal
¼ cup wheat germ
¼ cup tomato juice
¼ teaspoon sea salt

¼ teaspoon sage
¼ cup coarsely chopped celery
¼ cup coarsely chopped onions
¾ cup soy milk
1 egg

Place onion, celery, rice, oatmeal, wheat germ, soaked soybeans, sage, salt, egg, tomato juice, and soy milk in blender. Blend until well mixed. Pour blended ingredients into large bowl with ground meat. Mix well. Place mixture in oiled pan. Bake at 350 degrees for 45 minutes or until done. Serves 5 or 6.

Meat Loaf

Sauté lightly:
1 chopped onion
1 chopped green pepper or pimiento

1 minced clove garlic
1 teaspoon kelp

Remove from heat and add:
1 pound ground beef (mixed with heart and lung)
1 egg
½ cup wheat germ
2 tablespoons brewer's yeast

1 teaspoon sea salt
½ cup tomato juice
pinch each of thyme and basil
3 tablespoons ground parsley

127

Mix all ingredients thoroughly; mold into a loaf in a shallow baking dish or pack into an oiled loaf pan; sprinkle generously with paprika; bake in moderate oven at 350° F. about 40 minutes. Serves 5 or 6.

Meatballs, Millet and Mushroom Gravy

1 pound ground beef	1 tablespoon nutritional yeast
1 tablespoon vegetable oil	sea salt to taste
1 medium onion	1 cup of millet
2 cups water or stock	2 tablespoons arrowroot flour
1 pint mushrooms	

Chop onion fine and mix ½ into the meat, add sea salt and yeast. Mix well and form into 1-inch meatballs.

Brown in oil, then add the water and rest of the onion and mushrooms. Simmer half an hour.

Cook 1 cup of millet in 5 cups of boiling water for 20 minutes on medium high heat. Turn off heat, cover, and let stand until all the water is absorbed.

For the gravy, add 2 tablespoons arrowroot flour to 1 cup cold water. Stir until all is dissolved in the water. Then pour at once into the meatballs and mushrooms in the pan, stirring until it thickens. Serve the meatballs and mushroom gravy over the millet to 5 or 6.

Spanish Brown Rice and Meat

2 tablespoons oil	3 stalks celery (chopped)
1 pound lean chopped beef (hamburger, heart, lung mixture)	1 clove garlic (minced)
	½ cup brown rice (raw)
2 large onions (chopped)	1 cup water
1 large green pepper (chopped)	1 pint tomatoes (2 cups)
	sea salt, pepper to taste

Put oil in pan and brown meat and vegetables. Add rice and water and simmer for 30 minutes. Add tomatoes and seasoning, continuing cooking for about 30 minutes until rice is tender, adding more liquid if necessary. Serves 4 to 6.

Polynesian Pot Roast

1 3- to 4-pound beef chuck roast	4 carrots, cut lengthwise in 3- to 4-inch strips
1 large onion, sliced	½ pound garden spinach (cleaned and stems removed)
1 cup pineapple juice (unsweetened)	1 pint fresh mushrooms (sliced)
¼ cup soy sauce	
1½ teaspoons ground ginger	1 tablespoon cornstarch
¼ teaspoon sea salt	1 tablespoon nutritional yeast
1 cup diagonally sliced celery	

In shallow baking dish, cover meat with onion rings. Combine pineapple juice, soy sauce, ginger and ¼ teaspoon sea salt. Pour over meat. Let stand in pineapple mixture 1 hour at room temperature, turning meat once. Place meat and onions in Dutch oven, or any heavy pan. Pour pineapple mixture over; cover and simmer 2½ hours, or till meat is tender. Add celery and carrots. Sprinkle vegetables with sea salt; bring to boiling, then simmer 20 minutes, arranging spinach and mushrooms on top of meat. Simmer 10 minutes or till spinach is wilted and other vegetables are crisp and tender. Remove meat and vegetables to heated platter, keep hot. Skim fat from meat juices. Blend together ¼ cup cold water, cornstarch and yeast. Stir into juices, cook and stir till thickened and bubbly. Serves 6 to 8.

Health-Full Chop Suey

An economical main dish that's delicious and nutritious.

In a large pot:

Sauté lightly in 3 tablespoons corn oil for 5 minutes:
3 medium onions (chopped)
4 large stalks celery (sliced thin)

¾ pound sandwich steaks cut in 1-inch-wide strips (may be omitted if vegetable dish only is desired)

Then:

Add 1 pound fresh mung bean sprouts.
Cover with water to 1½ inches over all ingredients. (Water will provide gravy.) Simmer 1 hour, covered.

Mix:

2 tablespoons blackstrap molasses
⅓ cup soy sauce
3 tablespoons brewer's yeast (level) mixed with enough

cold water to make a smooth paste. Add to pot mixture, stir well. Simmer 20 more minutes.

Serve over brown rice. Add soy sauce to taste. Serves 4.
If desired, add last:

½ cup sliced mushrooms
½ cup water chestnuts

½ cup sliced Jerusalem artichokes

Sukiyaki

Have all the ingredients ready and make this dish at the table for delightful entertaining—Japanese style. You may want to use an electric frying pan or a small hot plate with a skillet. The following recipe will serve 6 to 8 people.

1 pound sirloin or flank roast (sliced paper thin)
1 bunch scallions
3 medium onions (cut in rings)
2 pounds spinach
½ pound mushrooms
1 celery cabbage
soy sauce
1 tablespoon blackstrap molasses

Ask your butcher to quick freeze the meat and slice it thin for you. Cut all the vegetables in bite size pieces and arrange with meat on a platter. Heat skillet and add oil; put in small amounts of all vegetables—start with onions, add scallions and spinach, mushrooms and celery cabbage. Add meat last. Sprinkle tablespoon blackstrap molasses over the mixture. Add enough soy sauce to cover the bottom of the pan to prevent burning.

In a short time the guests may start serving themselves in small cereal dishes provided at each place. Each guest is also served a bowl of brown rice at this time. The host should now refill the skillet so that another serving will be cooked by the time the guests are ready for more.

Yogurt Beef Stroganoff

1½ pounds beef fillet
4 tablespoons oil
3 cups mushrooms, thinly sliced
¾ cup onions, thinly sliced
sea salt
½ cup yogurt

Cut beef into narrow strips ½ × 2 inches. Season with sea salt and refrigerate 2 hours. Sauté beef quickly in oil, turning it so that it will brown evenly. In a separate pan sauté lightly in 2 tablespoons oil thinly sliced mushrooms and onions. Add meat. Season to taste with sea salt, kelp, and a grating of nutmeg. Add warmed yogurt. Reheat, being careful not to boil, and serve immediately. Serves 4.

Yogurt will not only enrich meats but the lactic acid it contains helps to soften or tenderize the connective tissue. Yogurt can be added to veal, pot roast, liver, chicken, lamb or to any braised meats.

Lamb on Brown Rice

1 tablespoon corn oil
2 pounds ground lamb
1 cup chopped onion
3 cups chopped celery and leaves
2 cups sliced mushrooms
1 green pepper (finely chopped)
3 cups soup stock (hot)
1 tablespoon kelp
1 tablespoon dried marjoram

Place all ingredients in heavy, hot Dutch oven. When celery is tender, thicken the mixture with rice polishings and add 1 teaspoon soy sauce. Serve over hot brown rice. Garnish with parsley. Serves 8 to 10.

Breast of Lamb
(stuffed with brown rice)

For each breast of lamb (ask butcher to make pocket for stuffing):

1 clove garlic

¾ cup brown rice, parboiled 15 minutes in salted water

2 tablespoons minced parsley

¼ cup chopped raw peanuts, pecans or any mixed nut combination

¾ teaspoon sea salt

4 tablespoons high protein flour mix (mixture of wheat germ, soy flour, peanut flour, nutritional yeast and rice polish. I keep this mix in a jar in refrigerator)

4 tablespoons oil

2 cups—water or soup stock

Trim fat from meat. Discard. Rub the cut clove of garlic into inside and outside of meat. Combine rice that has been drained (save the water), salt, chopped nuts and parsley. Fill pocket in breast of lamb and fasten opening with skewers or sew it up with strong white thread. Pat bottom and top with high protein flour mix. Heat oil in roasting pan and place filled breast in center, spooning some of the oil over top. Add two cups rice water or soup stock. Roast at 325 degrees allowing 30 to 35 minutes per pound of meat. Baste occasionally with the gravy in the pan. Serves 4 to 6.

Variation: Omit chopped nuts. Add one pound of chopped beef, prepared as for hamburger to ingredients listed. Proceed as in basic recipe. This serves 6 to 7 very heartily.

Pitchah—An Old World Favorite

This is one of the most body-warming, spirit-lifting dishes . . . wonderful for a bleak day when spirits are low and the budget stretched. You will need calves' feet which your friendly butcher will supply—washed and chopped. If he doesn't have feet, ask for veal knee and shin bones.

Cook these bones in water to cover with a chopped onion, salt, pepper and a clove of garlic, and 2 tablespoons distilled vinegar. Cook gently for almost 2 hours or until the cartilage comes away from the bones. Add more liquid if necessary. Now beat up an egg and add one tablespoon of lemon juice to it. Add a little hot liquid from the pot to the beaten egg and continue beating. Add this egg mixture to the pot.

Now—toast some stale bread in the oven—one slice for each person. When the toast is crunchy, rub both sides gently with garlic. Place a piece of this fragrant toast in each bowl and serve the bones and liquid broth on top.

Some people like to chop the cartilage and refrigerate for a gelatin salad. This is great for a buffet supper. Hard cooked eggs enhance this dish. Garnish with lemon slices.

Organ Meats

Piquant Lung and Heart

1 lb. calf or beef heart
1 pre-cooked lung (from soup)
3 tablespoons cold pressed oil
3 tablespoons onions chopped fine
2 tablespoons soy flour

1 cup tomato sauce or puree
½ teaspoon paprika
¼ cup lemon juice or apple cider vinegar
2 tablespoons blackstrap molasses or honey
1 cup stock or water

Heat oil. Brown onions and sprinkle with soy flour and paprika. Add diced heart and lung, tomato sauce or puree, vinegar or lemon juice and molasses or honey. Cover and cook over moderate heat for about half an hour. Add salt to taste and stock or water. Simmer for another half hour. Garnish with fresh parsley. Serves 5 or 6.

Beef Liver Creole

1 pound beef liver
3 tablespoons whole wheat or soy flour
1¼ cups sliced onions
1½ cups canned tomatoes

½ cup diced celery
1 thinly-sliced green pepper
½ teaspoon salt
few grains cayenne or paprika

Cut liver into thin slices. Dust with flour. Brown in oil or chicken fat. Add remaining ingredients. Cover and simmer for 20 minutes. Thicken gravy if necessary. Serve with boiled rice, noodles or cornmeal. Serves 4 or 5.

Chopped Liver

Cut up the liver you have left over from last night's dinner. Chop it with sautéed onions and any chicken cracklings (gribben) you may be storing in the freezer. Add a few lettuce leaves, a hard cooked egg, salt and fresh-ground pepper. The lettuce gives the liver a nice moist quality and precludes the addition of more fat. Sesame seeds are great

133

as a garnish on chopped liver. Chopped liver is delicious served on cucumber slices for those who don't want the calories you get in crackers—good stuffed in celery or on turnip slices—or served with lettuce and tomato as a salad.

Liver
(for people who don't like liver . . .)

A boy scout should always be cheerful—except when there's liver for dinner, our youngest son once maintained. Since his boy scout days, I've learned how to prepare liver so that even those who profess to hate the stuff—enjoy it. The secret is lemon juice and seasonings. Rub both sides of the liver with a cut lemon or sprinkle it all over with lemon juice. This is what cuts the livery taste some people find objectionable. Then coat it in a mixture of soy flour, yeast, kelp, paprika, a little crushed thyme and some sesame seeds.

Now, sauté some onions in a little oil or chicken fat. Remove onions to serve as a side dish with the potatoes, brown rice or Kasha you'll be serving as your starch dish. Now add about 2 tablespoons of oil to the pan and get it good and hot. Make sure that the family is about ready to come in for dinner before you put in the liver. Sear the liver slices for about three minutes on each side. It will be brown and crusty on the outside, tender and moist on the inside—and really good eating.

Applesauce, string beans and a tossed salad go great with liver.

P. S. Always prepare more liver than you need. Then you have some left over for chopped liver.

Liver Delight

2 cups cubed liver	2 cups finely chopped cabbage
2 tablespoons cooking oil	1 cup finely chopped onions
3 tablespoons soy flour	1 cup chopped, fresh tomatoes

Cut liver in one-fourth-inch cubes and toss with soy flour till coated. Place skillet on lowest heat. Add liver and oil. Simmer till liver is tender. Use a tight fitting lid. When the liver is no longer red, add the vegetables and a dash of kelp and garlic. Let simmer till vegetables are tender but not over-cooked. Serves 4.

Raw Liver Pattie

Cut beef liver in small pieces for easier handling. Then dip in hot water to stiffen enough for grinding, but do not cook. Grind, or chop liver. Mix with an equal amount of mashed potatoes, a little chopped onion and green pepper. Also add a little garlic, if you like, and a little sea salt or kelp. Make small patties about the size of a good-sized cookie. Pace in the freezer. Just warm them for serving. The onion and pepper could be cooked a little if desired.

Liver Veal Loaf

½ pound beef liver
1 pint boiling water
1 medium onion, lightly sautéed in chicken fat or oil
1½ pounds boneless veal, ground, or you could use your hamburger-heart-lung mixture

2 eggs, (slightly beaten)
1 cup tomato sauce
½ cup wheat germ (or more)
⅛ teaspoon sage
sea salt to taste

In a bowl, pour the boiling water over the liver and let stand for 10 minutes. Drain off the water and cut the liver coarsely. Grind liver with the onion, using a medium blade. Combine with the ground veal. Add tomato sauce, seasonings, eggs and wheat germ. Mix thoroughly and pack into an oiled loaf pan. Bake in a moderate oven for 1½ hours. Serve hot or cold to 5 or 6.

Lung and Beef Stew

1 beef lung (cut into small pieces)
1 pound of lean beef
3 tablespoons chicken fat or oil
1 clove garlic (minced)
3 medium onions (diced)

1½ cups stewed tomatoes
1 tablespoon honey
½ cup soup stock or hot water —if necessary
sea salt and paprika to taste
1 tablespoon yeast

Sauté meat, add garlic and onions. Cook one hour. Add tomatoes, honey and remaining ingredients. A tablespoon of food yeast will enhance the flavor. This is great served with brown rice. Serves 6 or 8.

Milt or spleen, like other glandular meats, is rich in good protein and outstandingly rich in B vitamins and iron. Use it the same way you use brains and sweetbreads, add it to heart and lung in a stew, or to a beef goulash.

Stuffed Milt

1 beef milt (cut for stuffing)
1 clove garlic (minced)
4 onions (sliced)

½ teaspoon sea salt
2 tablespoons oil

Filling

1½ cups brown rice or kasha
1 egg
1 onion, diced
2 tablespoons oil
¼ teaspoon poultry seasoning

¼ cup chopped peanuts or pecans
dash of ginger
some chopped parsley

Have your butcher make an incision into the side of the milt. Prepare the milt for cooking by trimming away particles of fat. Combine ingredients for filling in a bowl. Stuff into incision and secure with skewers or sew it together. Place stuffed milt on bed of garlic and onions in roasting pan. Prick in several places with fork to prevent curling up at the edges. Roast at 350 degrees about 50 minutes or till the top is brown.

Fried Sweetbreads

Cook prepared sweetbreads as for broiling. Remove membrane and slice. Dip both sides in slightly salted soy flour, wheat germ or sesame seeds. Sauté in hot melted chicken or goose fat or oil till nicely browned on both sides. Garnish with minced parsley or fresh dill.

Two pairs of sweetbreads will serve 4 nicely.

Sautéed Sweetbreads with Mushrooms

2 pairs beef sweetbreads, parboiled as for broiling
2 tablespoons oil
2 tablespoons soy flour or wheat germ
1 cup sliced fresh mushrooms or 1 small can button mushrooms

1 tablespoon onion juice
dash of soy sauce
salt and paprika to taste
2 hard cooked eggs, sliced or diced
2 tablespoons minced parsley

Trim parboiled sweetbreads of membrane. Dice and sauté in hot oil 10 minutes over moderate heat. Dust with flour or wheat germ; add mushrooms, onion juice, soy sauce and seasonings and cover. Simmer 20 minutes over moderate heat. Serve with sliced hard-cooked eggs and parsley garnish.

Serves 4.

Ruthie's "Hearty" Veal Stew

1 large veal heart	½ bay leaf
1 pound veal neck bones	oregano, marjoram, thyme,
1 medium onion	pepper
2 carrots	1 teaspoon brewer's yeast
2 potatoes	1 tablespoon oil
1 yam	

Scrub potatoes and yam and peel carrots. Cut into quarters. Rinse heart and dry. Cut into stew size pieces with poultry utility scissors. Dice onion and sauté in oil. Add the meat and brown on all sides. Add water to cover and seasonings. Bring to a boil and simmer about 2 hours. Add vegetables and continue to simmer till everything is tender, about another hour. Thicken gravy with yeast. Serves 2.

Great Fish Recipes

Try to get your fish from Iceland where there is reputedly less pollution. Since pollutants in today's environment are inescapable, I serve the best food I can find and then make sure my family gets plenty of vitamins C, B, and E so each one is better equipped to detoxify those poisons we cannot avoid.

Easy Fish Chowder

½ cup thinly diced celery
2 tablespoons oil
¼ teaspoon sea salt
4 boiled potatoes

½ cup diced cooked carrots
½ cup soy milk
½ cup water
1 cup flaked cooked haddock

Cook celery in oil until tender. Add sea salt and remaining ingredients. Heat, cooking until bubbly.
Serve with sprinkling of chopped parsley. Serves 4.

Onion-Apple Stuffed Cod

1 pound fresh cod fillets
1 tablespoon cold-pressed oil
¼ cup finely-chopped onion
2 tablespoons finely-chopped celery
¾ cup chopped apple

3 tablespoons finely-chopped fresh parsley
⅛ teaspoon sea salt
1/16 teaspoon thyme
1 tablespoon lemon juice
paprika

Heat oil in skillet and sauté onion and celery until soft. Stir in apple, parsley, sea salt, thyme and lemon juice. Mix until well blended. In a shallow baking dish (lightly oiled) lay one-half of the fish fillets. Spoon stuffing mixture over the entire surface. Lay remaining fillet over the stuffing. Drizzle top with oil and sprinkle with paprika. Bake in a 400 degree oven for about 20 minutes or until fish flakes easily with the tines of a fork. Serve hot to 2 or 3.

138

Flounder with Mushroom Sauce

3 pounds flounder fillets
½ cup water
1 tablespoon butter
2 tablespoons soy flour
½ cup canned mushrooms (chopped)

1 sprig sweet basil
½ teaspoon allspice
1 sprig thyme
2 sprigs parsley
1 bay leaf
sea salt and paprika to taste

Rub fish with sea salt and paprika. Bake with ½ cup water at 375° for 25 minutes. Remove from oven. Melt butter, add flour, and stir until smooth. Remove from heat and add remaining ingredients and liquid from fish. Cook over low heat, stirring constantly until thickened. Score top of fish, pour sauce over fish, and bake in oven 15 minutes longer. Serves 6.

Halibut Pilaf

½ tablespoon safflower oil
¼ cup chopped green pepper
¼ cup chopped celery
½ cup brown rice
2 tablespoons minced onion

½ cup cold water
2 cups tomatoes
sea salt and paprika to taste
2 cups cooked halibut, cut into chunks

Heat the oil in a large, heavy skillet. Add pepper, celery, rice and onion, stirring constantly for fifteen minutes. Add water, tomatoes and seasonings and stir until well blended. Add halibut chunks and stir for five minutes. Transfer to an oiled casserole. Cover tightly and bake in a slow oven until rice is tender. Serve hot to 3 or 4.

Chopped Herring

1 large pickled herring
1 large onion
1 medium sour apple

3 hard boiled eggs
crackers to thicken
vinegar to taste

Grind all ingredients together in food chopper. Serve as a dip or spread.

Salmon Loaf

(2 to 3 servings)

½ pound can salmon
1 beaten egg
⅓ cup soy powder
¼ teaspoon sea salt

⅓ cup soy milk
1 teaspoon rose hip powder
1 tablespoon wheat germ

Sift soy powder, salt, rose hip powder and wheat germ. Combine beaten egg and milk and gradually stir into dry mixture. Break salmon into small pieces and add with juice. Bake in greased, small loaf pan in moderate oven (350° F) until loaf is firm (about 1 hour). Serves 2 or 3.

Mrs. Bunn's Swordfish Banana Cake

swordfish (at least one inch thick)
nut milk or soy milk (thick)

wheat germ or sesame seeds
bananas sliced lengthwise
lemon juice

Dip fish in milk, then in sesame seeds or wheat germ (both sides). Place on oiled cookie sheet; put bananas on top. Sprinkle lemon juice over fish and bananas. Bake at 450° for about 15 to 20 minutes, depending on thickness of fish. This dish needs no other seasoning. Serve with parsleyed potatoes, steamed broccoli and a tossed salad and you have a gourmet meal.

Breakfast

"Old Soak" Powerhouse Cereal

You don't have to rely on store-bought, empty-calorie cereals. You can make your own good stuff. It's quick, easy and gratifying.

The night before, put the following to soak in cold water:

½ cup chopped sunflower seeds
½ cup millet

1 cup unsprayed unsulphured raisins or dried prunes
½ cup large rolled oats
½ cup buckwheat groats

In the morning, put the cereal (adding more water if needed) on a moderate heat and bring to a boil. Serve with nut milk. It needs no sweetener as the fruit gives it a natural sweetness. This serves 4 hearty eaters.

Golden Millet Cereal

Discover millet. It is considered to be the best of all the grains by many nutritionists. It is an excellent source of calcium, iron and protein. It makes a wonderful breakfast food.

1 cup whole millet
1 teaspoon sea salt

1 quart water

Combine ingredients in top part of a double boiler. Place over direct heat and boil for about 5 minutes. Then move to top of the bottom section containing hot water. Simmer for about a half hour. Serve hot. Four to six servings.

You can use millet in any recipe that calls for cornmeal.

Granola Cereal Mix

If you are blessed with a large family, prepare your own granola by the gallon.

Mix lightly in a bowl:

½ cup sunflower seed meal or any nut meal
1 cup corn flour
3 quarts oatmeal
½ cup chopped unsulphured dates or figs
½ cup chopped sun dried, seedless unsulphured raisins

½ cup unsweetened coconut
½ cup soya flour
1 cup stone-ground cornmeal
1 cup chopped nuts (such as pecans, walnuts or peanuts)
½ cup seeds such as sesame, sunflower or pumpkin
¼ cup wheat germ

Then mix:
½ cup date sugar
1⅓ cups water
⅔ cup raw honey

1⅓ cups cold-pressed sesame seed oil

Combine mixtures. It should be moist, chunky, and crumbly. If too moist, add more oatmeal.

Spread thin on cookie sheet. Bake 1 hour at 225° F. or until light brown. Makes approximately 1 gallon.

Serve with warm homemade applesauce to which a dash of cinnamon has been added, or with any chopped or sliced fresh fruit or canned fruit. Serve as a cold cereal with soy milk or nut milk.

Buckwheat (Kasha) Delight

Here's a breakfast dish that's festive enough to double as dessert.

To 2½ cups boiling water add ½ cup buckwheat groats. Sweeten to taste with honey and add raisins and chopped dates. Boil for about 12 minutes. When almost finished, stir in ½ cup shredded coconut.

This is delicious served hot or cold. Serves 4.

Apple Muesli

2 tablespoons old-fashioned oatmeal
2 tablespoons wheat germ
½ lemon (juiced)
1 tablespoon raisins (unsulphured)

2 apples
2 tablespoons raw honey
2 tablespoons walnuts (chopped) or sunflower seeds
½ cup yogurt

Soak oatmeal overnight in four tablespoons of pure water. In the morning, add lemon juice and yogurt, mix well. Grate apples, unpeeled if they are unsprayed, into the mixture. Add remaining ingredients. Mix it all up and enjoy immediately. Serves 1.

Variations of this dish are a favorite at the famous Bircher-Benner clinic in Switzerland. You can enjoy it every day in your own home.

Fig Muesli

In the blender, put the following and whiz fine:

3 cups warm water
1 carrot, cut in chunks
1 cup unblanched almonds

3 unsprayed apples, cored
   and cut in chunks
1 cup stemmed dried figs

This can be made quicker if you put the carrot and almonds and 1 cup of water in the blender first, reduce it to fine pulp, then add the rest of the ingredients. Cover the blender tightly while whizzing, to keep the air out. Sprinkle with sunflower seed meal. Serves 3 or 4.

Barley Pancakes

Nothin' says lovin' at breakfast time like hot nutritious pancakes that stick to your ribs.

Pour ½ cup warm water into mixing bowl. Add 2 tablespoons of baker's yeast, 2 tablespoons of honey and let rise for 30 minutes, in a warm place. Add:

2 eggs
1 cup soy milk
1 cup raw wheat germ

1 cup barley flour
2 tablespoons vegetable oil

Mix well and bake on a moderately hot griddle until done. Spread with cashew butter and top with honey or pure maple syrup. Serves 4.

Soy-Corn Waffles

2 eggs, separated
1 teaspoon sea kelp
1 cup sifted corn flour
4 tablespoons cooking oil

2 cups soy or nut milk
1 cup sifted soy low-fat flour
1 tablespoon sunflower seed
   meal

Beat the egg whites very stiff and set aside. Beat the other ingredients well, fold in the egg whites and bake in waffle iron until crisp. This will make 5 or 6 waffles on round iron.

French Toast

½ cup soy or nut milk
3 eggs
1 teaspoon sea salt
6 slices stale, whole grain
   bread (preferably
   homemade)

½ cup wheat germ
1 tablespoon blackstrap
   molasses (optional)
dash of cinnamon

Soak the bread in a mixture of the other ingredients until it is soft. Sauté slowly in butter or oil until brown on both sides.

Serve with applesauce or with yogurt.

When I taught a class in cooking to a group of 10-year-olds, they loved making and eating French toast made this way. The molasses makes the mixture dark but gives it a sweet tang that children love.

When you're in a class setting, you don't have to be sneaky with the wheat germ.

Whenever we made anything that called for flour, I would ask the class, "Now, what can we put in here to give it extra go-power?"

All hands would fly up and there would be a chorus of "Wheat Germ."

Protein Energy Omelet

This egg dish for breakfast will give your family a head-start.

Allow 2 eggs per person.

Beat 2 eggs with 1 teaspoon wheat germ, 1 teaspoon soy powder, and 1 teaspoon of mixed chopped chia seeds, sunflower seeds and sesame. (Keep a jar of these three seeds in the refrigerator, and run them through the blender.)

Add garlic powder and sea salt to taste and cook in oil. Try a little honey over it for a nice change.

Egg Foo Yung

6 large eggs
2 cups bean sprouts
2 small onions, chopped
2 tablespoons soy sauce
½ teaspoon sea salt

1 cup chopped chicken
2 cups steamed brown rice
parsley and mushrooms
 (optional, but very good)

Beat eggs. Add all ingredients but rice. Blend lightly.

Heat a small amount of oil in large heavy skillet. Pour in portions (pancake size). Brown and turn. Serve with hot steamed rice to which soy sauce has been added. This dish whether made with chicken or tuna always gets raves. Serves 6.

Desserts

Baking Hints

You will find no recipes here calling for baking soda and baking powder. Baking soda destroys some of the B vitamins. Baking powders contain baking soda. Most baking powders also contain alum which destroys certain vitamins and can cause gastric distress.

Bake with yeast and with extra egg whites to get a light airy quality in your baked goods. Egg whites should be beaten stiff and added last. Make sure your baking utensils are warm.

I use no hydrogenated fats—only vegetable oils.

I use honey, raw sugar, date sugar, maple syrup, blackstrap molasses or sorghum molasses in place of white sugar and corn syrup.

I use this high-protein flour in many recipes: Combine 4 cups whole wheat flour, 1 cup soy flour, ½ cup peanut flour, ¼ cup brown rice flour, ¼ cup brewer's yeast.

Carolyn's Apple Cake

½ cup corn oil
½ cup raw sugar
2 eggs, unbeaten
½ teaspoon vanilla
½ cup high protein pastry flour
½ teaspoon kelp
½ cup soy flour less 1 tablespoon

1 tablespoon rice polish (available from health food store)
grated peel of ½ lemon
3 red apples
⅓ cup date sugar
1 teaspoon cinnamon
2 tablespoons soy oil

Beat oil and ½ cup sugar until light and fluffy. Beat in eggs one at a time. Add vanilla. Mix and sift flour and kelp; add with rice polish and grated lemon peel. Beat well; spoon into greased 8-inch-square cake pan. Cut apples into quarters and remove core; cut each section into 4 slices (16 slices per apple). Place, peel side up, in rows in cake batter. Combine remaining ⅓ cup sugar and cinnamon; sprinkle over apples. Dot with oil. Bake at 350 degrees for about 45 minutes. Makes 6 servings.

Banana Nut Loaf

2 cups soy flour
½ teaspoon brewer's yeast
½ teaspoon sea salt
½ cup safflower or soy oil
1 cup honey

2 eggs, beaten
3 mashed bananas
3 tablespoons soy milk
½ teaspoon vanilla

Blend all ingredients. Turn into a greased loaf pan. Bake at 350° F. for one hour. Loaf will be moist—more like pudding than cake.

Carob Honey Cake

1½ cups wheat germ flour
⅓ cup carob
2 teaspoons cinnamon
1 teaspoon kelp
6 egg yolks
6 egg whites, beaten stiff

⅓ cup water
½ cup oil
1¼ cups honey
2 teaspoons pure vanilla
1 cup raisins

Sift dry ingredients into large bowl. Add oil, honey, egg yolks, vanilla and water. Beat egg whites in small bowl until stiff. Set aside. Beat first mixture 4 minutes at high speed with electric mixer. Add raisins, then fold in egg whites. Bake at 350° for an hour.

Nuts or sunflower seeds may be added.

Sunflower Date Loaf Cake

1 yeast cake
1 cup lukewarm water
¾ cup chopped seeded dates
½ cup date sugar or raw honey
2 beaten egg yolks

¾ cup sunflower seeds, coarsely chopped
½ teaspoon sea salt
½ teaspoon cloves
1 teaspoon cinnamon
2½ cups high protein flour (see baking hints)

Dissolve yeast in water, add 1 cup flour and mix until spongy. Let rise until light and frothy. Add and blend into sponge remaining ingredients. This becomes a fairly firm loaf. Spoon into greased loaf pan or bread tin, let rise until nearly doubled, bake at 375° at least 45 minutes.

Carob Brownies

Have three sizes of mixing bowls. Mix as follows:

In large bowl:

½ cup honey
2 tablespoons blackstrap
  molasses

¼ cup sunflower seed oil
2 eggs separated. Beat yolks,
  add to mixture

In small bowl:
Beat the whites; set aside

In medium bowl:

½ cup soybean powder
½ cup sunflower seed meal
½ cup carob powder
½ teaspoon allspice
  (optional)

½ teaspoon ginger
  (optional)
1 teaspoon cinnamon
  (optional)
1 teaspoon pure vanilla can
  be used in place of spices

Now add this mixture to large bowl, a little at a time. This will be very stiff.

Add:

½ cup of chopped raisins or
dates; mix well.

Add the whites of eggs (beaten
  stiff but not dry)

Pour into oiled 9-inch-square pan. Bake in oven heated to 350° for 25 minutes. Cool; cut into squares.

Sesame Strips (Brownie's)

Our family fell in love with these when we dined at Brownie's in New York. Sam Brown very graciously gave me the recipe. You'll love 'em.

1¾ cups raw sugar
1 cup soybean oil
3 tablespoons skim milk
  powder
2 eggs
1 tablespoon pure vanilla
¼ cup wheat germ
½ cup sesame seeds

½ cup cashews coarsely
  chopped
1 cup unsulphured raisins
½ cup water
6 cups high protein flour mix
  (4 cups whole wheat, 1 cup
  soy, ½ cup peanut flour, ¼
  cup brown rice flour, ¼ cup
  nutritional yeast)

Combine sugar, soybean oil and skim milk powder; mix for 2 minutes. Add eggs and vanilla; mix for 2 minutes. Add wheat germ, sesame seeds, cashews and raisins; mix 3 minutes. Add water and flour (you may need more water) and mix until smooth ball of dough is formed. Let dough rest 10 minutes. Divide into 4 equal pieces. Roll each piece on lightly floured (whole wheat flour) surface to 16 inches. Transfer to greased baking sheet. Flatten each strip to 5 inches in width. Brush with egg wash (beat up egg with a little water). Sprinkle generously with sesame seeds. Bake at 300° for 45 minutes. Cut diagonally into 1-inch strips. Yield: 64 strips.

Peanut-Raisin Cookies
Crunchy cookies—without baking powder

½ cup wheat germ
½ cup soy flour
2½ cups oatmeal
1 tablespoon baking yeast
½ teaspoon sea salt
¾ cup chopped raw peanuts
2 eggs

⅓ cup vegetable oil
⅔ cup honey or blackstrap molasses
½ cup apple or pineapple juice
1 teaspoon pure vanilla
½ cup raisins

Mix dry ingredients well (wheat germ, soy flour, oatmeal, yeast, sea salt, chopped peanuts).

In a large bowl beat together oil, honey or molasses; add eggs, beat again. Then add juice, vanilla and raisins. Mix well. Add dry ingredients to liquid mixture and mix well. Let batter rest 20 minutes before baking. Drop by teaspoons onto oiled cookie sheets. Bake at 375° 10-15 minutes or until golden brown.

Tahini Cookies
(no flour)

6 tablespoons tahini (sesame seed butter)
½ cup raw honey
½ teaspoon cinnamon

½ cup chopped walnuts or chopped peanuts
1½ cups oatmeal (minute)

Stir honey and tahini together. Add nuts. Add oatmeal mixed with cinnamon till blended. Drop by teaspoons on oiled cookie sheet. Bake at 350° for about 10 minutes or until edges are brown. As a variation, add chopped apples, raisins or dates.

Soy Walnut Cookies

½ cup honey
½ cup blackstrap molasses
4 egg yolks
4 egg whites, beaten

1 cup raisins
2 cups broken walnuts
¾ cup soy flour
1 tablespoon cinnamon

Cream honey, molasses, yolks; fold in raisins, walnuts, and flour and cinnamon. Fold in beaten egg white. Spread on oiled cookie sheet. Bake 20 minutes—350° oven. Cut in strips when cool.

Carrot and Nut Cake
(the cake you bake without flour)

5 eggs, separated
¾ cup raw sugar
1 teaspoon vanilla
¼ teaspoon sea salt
¼ pound carrots, grated

½ pound almonds, finely
  grated or blended in
  electric blender
¼ cup wheat germ
2 teaspoons nutritional yeast

Blend together egg yolks and sugar. Add vanilla, salt and yeast and beat until light and fluffy. Stir in grated carrots, nuts and wheat germ. Fold in stiffly beaten whites. Bake in lightly greased 9-inch spring form pan for one hour at 350° or until cake springs back when pressed with finger. Cool in pan.

Date Torte

This recipe was developed at Fitness House, the Rodale Press dining room Preheat oven to 325° F.

4 eggs, separated
½ cup honey
1 cup walnuts, chopped fine
1 cup chopped dates
¼ cup coconut shreds

½ cup rice flour
¼ teaspoon sea salt
1 tablespoon lemon juice
1 teaspoon lemon rind

1. Prepare a nine-inch-square pan by oiling bottom of pan with pastry brush. Cut a piece of heavy brown paper to fit bottom of pan; brush with oil and set to one side.
2. Put egg whites in large bowl of electric mixer. With mixer set at high speed, beat whites until stiff peaks form when beater is slowly raised. Set aside. With same beater, beat yolks until thick and lemon-colored. Gradually add honey, beating at low speed.
3. Stir in chopped nuts and lemon juice. Add coconut and lemon rind.
4. Measure and sift rice flour and salt. Add chopped dates to flour mixture and coat evenly. Stir into mixture.
5. Fold yolk mixture into beaten egg whites until well combined.
6. Pour the batter into the prepared pan, spreading evenly to edges. Bake for 25 minutes.
7. Remove from oven and invert pan on wire rack. Remove paper from cake immediately and allow to cool before serving. Note: This cake may be served plain or with a basic lemon sauce, using cornstarch, lemon juice and honey.

Pineapple Nut Torte

5 large eggs, separated
½ cup raw honey
1½ cups wheat germ

3 cups ground nuts (walnuts
   or pecans)
20-ounce can unsweetened,
   crushed pineapple

Beat yolks until light, add honey, beat again. Add wheat germ and nuts, beat. Add crushed pineapple, stir. Fold in stiffly beaten egg whites. Bake at 325° for 30 minutes in two greased cake pans or in one large, greased, baking pan.

Non-Wheat Pastry

For a 9- or 10-inch double crust pie, the amounts are as follows:

2 cups flour: mixture of rice,
   soy, potato
¾ teaspoon sea salt

⅔ cup sunflower seed oil
3 tablespoons nut milk

Combine flour and salt in pie plate. Add "milk" to oil and beat with fork. Add milk-oil mixture to flour and combine with fork until all flour is moistened. For double crust reserve one third of mixture. Spread and press remaining mixture to cover sides and bottom of pan evenly. Fill as desired. Top with remaining third crumbled evenly over surface. Bake at 400° for 15 minutes, reduce heat to 350° and bake till filling is cooked (about 30 minutes for fruit).

No Bake, No Sugar Fruit Pie
(dessert)

1 pound raisins, ground up,
   and rind of one organically
   grown orange
¼ cup honey

1 teaspoon cinnamon
⅛ teaspoon cloves
1 cup nut meats

Press in pie plate after all ingredients are well mixed (double it if you prefer large pie). No crust. Tastes even better after a few days.

Sweet Potato Almond Crustless Pie

1½ cups mashed sweet
   potatoes
3 tablespoons oil
½ cup honey
3 eggs, separated

few grains salt
1 teaspoon cinnamon
⅓ cup chopped almonds
1½ cups nut milk

Combine sweet potatoes, oil and honey. Beat egg yolks, and add. Add salt, cinnamon and mix thoroughly. Add almonds with milk to first mixture. Beat egg whites stiff and fold in. Pour into oiled pie plate. Bake in hot oven, 425° F., 15 minutes. Reduce heat to moderately hot, 375° F. Bake 25 minutes longer, or until firm. Cool. Top with yogurt and additional almonds if desired.

Tip: Rub the baking utensil with liquid lecithin and you won't have to oil it. You can make any pan non-stick by the same technique.

Apple Rice Betty

4 large tart apples
1 cup cooked brown rice
½ cup chopped walnuts
1 cup honey

¼ teaspoon cloves
¼ teaspoon cinnamon
¼ teaspoon sea salt
2 tablespoons oil

Mix honey with spices. Grease baking dish. Place a thin layer of rice in dish; add a layer of thinly sliced apples, and sprinkle with honey, spices and nuts. Repeat layers until all ingredients are used, saving some honey and nuts for the top. Pour oil over all.

Bake in 350° oven until apples are soft. Serve hot.

Raspberry Supreme

1 cup cooked brown rice (hot)
1 cup nut milk

2 eggs
1 tablespoon honey
1 cup raspberries

Mix first four ingredients together and cook on low heat until thick, stirring constantly. Add 1 cup fresh or frozen berries. Serve hot or cold.

Vanilla Rice Custard

3 tablespoons cooked brown rice
1 cup nut milk or soy milk
1 egg, slightly beaten

3 tablespoons honey
1 teaspoon pure vanilla
½ cup raisins

Mix well and sprinkle cinnamon over top. Bake at 325° about one hour or until silver knife comes out clean.

Pineapple Pudding

¼ cup cold-pressed oil
3 to 4 cups crushed pineapple (unsweetened)
½ cup honey
1 teaspoon cinnamon

1 cup wheat germ
½ cup pumpkin seeds (ground)
1 cup coconut (unsweetened)
2 tablespoons soybean oil

Combine oil, pineapple, honey and cinnamon. Combine wheat

germ and ground seeds. Put half of pineapple mixture into a 1½ quart shallow baking dish. Sprinkle with half of wheat germ and ground seeds mixture, and half of coconut. Repeat layers. Dot with oil. Sprinkle with remaining coconut. Bake at 350° F. for 15 minutes. Serve warm or cold. Serves 8-10.

Coconut Mousse
(an elegant, refreshing dessert)

Dissolve 1 level tablespoon gelatin in ¼ cup cold water. In a small saucepan combine 2 egg yolks, ⅓ cup honey, ½ cup coconut meat and ½ cup coconut milk. Blend and cook gently about 2 minutes, then stir in and melt the gelatin mixture. Cool. Add 1 teaspoon pure vanilla and 2 stiffly beaten egg whites. Pour in oiled mold and chill.

Yogurt-Fruit Dessert

For each person to be served, allow:

½ banana, firm, ripe	1 tablespoon grated natural
⅛ cup fruit juice (pineapple,	coconut
or other naturally sweet	1 tablespoon ground sun-
juice)	flower seeds (medium fine)
½ cup thick yogurt	1 tablespoon wheat germ

Mash the banana with a fork. Add other ingredients and stir together till lightly blended. Serve in individual compote dishes. Variations:

(1) Use ½ ripe mealy type apple (if fruit is large) such as a golden Delicious, instead of banana. If apples are small, use 1 whole apple. Shred the apple or chop coarsely.

(2) Ripe peaches, sliced; strawberries, partly mashed, partly sliced; or other fresh fruit in season may be used instead of the banana. If canned fruit is used, drain off the juice.

Soy Whipped Cream

½ cup soy or cashew milk	¼ teaspoon vanilla
½ cup oil	pinch of sea salt or kelp
1 tablespoon honey	

Put milk and vanilla in blender. Slowly add the oil till mixture gets very thick. If necessary, add a little more oil. Blend in honey and salt.
Variations:
1. Use a few dates, figs or raisins instead of honey.
2. Omit vanilla and stir in ¼ cup fresh or frozen berries.
3. Add 2 teaspoons carob powder for the taste of chocolate cream.

Strawberry Filled Avocados with Minted French Dressing

2 medium avocados, cut in half, remove stones
3 tablespoons salad oil
1 tablespoon apple cider vinegar
½ teaspoon sea salt
¼ teaspoon paprika

1 cup fresh pineapple, cut to bite size pieces
1 pint strawberries
1 teaspoon honey
2 tablespoons minced, fresh mint leaves

Put salad dressing ingredients into jar with tight-fitting lid. Shake vigorously to mix or whiz in blender. Sprinkle one teaspoon dressing over each half ripe avocado. Fill centers of avocados with pineapple pieces and strawberries. Dress fruit with freshly shaken dressing and serve either as a salad course or combination dessert-salad. Serves 4.

Popcorn Balls

1 cup honey
1 teaspoon vanilla

¼ cup water
bowl of freshly popped corn

Put honey and water together. Put on high heat, stirring constantly till it boils. Change heat to medium and stir. When part of the mixture forms a ball in cold water, remove pan from heat. Mix in vanilla. Pour over popcorn and form balls. Roll in ground nuts, wheat germ or sesame seeds.

Sesame Treats

½ cup finely ground coconut (unsweetened)
½ cup sunflower seed meal
½ cup natural wheat germ

¼ cup tahini (ground sesame seed)
¼ cup honey

Mix all together.
Separate into two portions. Place each on a piece of waxed paper and form into a one-inch roll. Wrap in the paper and keep in the refrigerator. Cut into one-inch pieces as needed.

Fruit Candies

1 cup dried apricots
½ cup raisins
1 cup figs

¼ cup honey or sorghum molasses
1 cup raw peanuts
½ cup sunflower seeds

Grind fruits and nuts together. Use enough honey or molasses to bind the mixture. Roll walnut-sized balls in sesame seeds.

Roll-Ups

1 cup raw wheat germ
½ cup soy grits
1 cup soy lecithin granules
½ cup date sugar
½ cup raw honey
1 cup carob powder
1 cup grated fresh coconut

½ cup sesame or sunflower seed oil
2 teaspoons pure vanilla
1½ cups chopped dates
1 cup seedless raisins
1 cup sunflower meal or sesame meal or almond meal

Mix dry ingredients; combine oil, honey and vanilla. Add to dry mixture. Add dates, raisins, coconut and sesame meal. Mix with enough pure water to be able to lightly knead the mixture. Divide in thirds. Sprinkle coconut on sheet of wax paper and shape into 1½ × 10 inch roll. Store the rolls in the refrigerator. Then cut small portions off and roll to make individual tootsie rolls.

Potato Carob Bonbons

2 cups cold mashed potatoes
2 tablespoons carob powder
¼ teaspoon kelp powder
1 cup medium ground coconut
1 tablespoon honey

1 teaspoon vanilla
1 teaspoon liquid lecithin (optional)
⅛ teaspoon ginger
¼ cup chopped dates
1 tablespoon rice polish
finely ground coconut

Combine thoroughly the potatoes, carob powder and kelp, using wooden spoon. Add remaining ingredients, in order given, and mix well.

Dough should become of consistency to handle with fingers; if too moist, add more rice polish.

Shape into bite-size balls and roll in finely ground coconut. Refrigerate for about 8 hours before using. Makes about 40 bonbons.

Ice Cream and Other Frozen Desserts

Ice cream manufacturers are not required by law to list the additives used in the manufacture of their product. Consequently, all but a few brands of ice cream are synthetic from start to finish. A breakdown of ingredients commonly used to make commercial ice cream has shown the following: Piperonal, a de-lousing chemical, is used in place of vanilla. Ethyl acetate is used to give ice cream a pineapple flavor—a cleaner for leather and textiles, its vapors have been known to cause chronic lung, liver and heart damage. Amyl acetate, a solvent for oil paint, is used for banana flavor.

You don't have to feed your family chemicals. You can make your own ice cream.

Vanilla Ice Cream

I learned this method from *Ten Talents,* an excellent book by Dr. Frank Hurd and his wife, Rosalie. It holds its shape and requires only one freezing.

Soak 1 tablespoon agar-agar flakes (you can get them from Walnut Acres, Penns Creek, Pennsylvania) in one cup of water. Boil one minute and cool one minute.

Add:

1 cup cashews	½ cup raw honey
2 cups water	⅓ cup oil (soy)
3 tablespoons soy-milk powder	1 tablespoon vanilla
	¼ teaspoon sea salt

Liquefy the first three ingredients in the blender till very smooth. Add honey, vanilla and salt. Blend again. Add oil slowly while blending. Blend one minute more. Freeze in tray. Serve before it gets too hard.

If you don't have agar-agar on hand, but do have slippery elm powder, try this method:

Blend till smooth:

1 cup cashews	1 teaspoon slippery elm
3 cups water	

Add slowly:

½ cup raw honey	1-2 tablespoons soy-milk powder (optional)
⅓ cup soy or coconut oil	
1 tablespoon vanilla	¼ teaspoon sea salt

Blend well and freeze. Whip again and return to freezer.

Raspberry Ice Cream

Place the following ingredients in a liquefier in the order listed:

1 large can evaporated milk, chilled	3 egg yolks
4 tablespoons raw honey	1 pint raspberries

Combine ingredients in blender and run machine for three minutes. Pour into mixing bowl. Then whip in the liquefier the following:

1 pint whipping cream   1 pint raspberries

Fold this mixture into the milk mixture. Then beat and fold in three egg whites. Pour into freezing trays and freeze. For best results, beat mixture at several intervals during the freezing time.

Strawberry Honey Ice Cream

2 eggs, separated   1 pint strawberries, thor-
1 cup honey, warmed   oughly mashed
1 pint whipping cream

Beat the two egg yolks well and mix with cup of warmed honey. Whip the cream and combine with the mashed strawberries. Add this mixture to the egg and honey mixture and blend well. Pour into freezing tray and freeze for about an hour. At this point fold in two egg whites, beaten until stiff, and continue freezing. Beat mixture every thirty minutes during freezing time to insure a smooth ice cream.

Pumpkin Ice Cream

1 cup cooked pumpkin   ½ cup condensed milk
½ cup natural brown sugar   4 tablespoons honey
   (optional)   10 marshmallows

Combine liquids in electric mixer bowl. Gradually add solids while machine is running (about two minutes). Pour into freezer trays and freeze until soft and mushy. Pour into chilled bowl and beat again until smooth. Pour back into freezer trays and refreeze until firm, stirring at frequent intervals.

Cantaloupe Sherbet

1½ cups water   3 cups fresh cantaloupe pulp
½ cup date sugar or honey   and juice

Boil water and sugar together for about five minutes so that sugar dissolves. Add cantaloupe pulp and juice and mix well. Pour into freezer tray and freeze.

Date Ice Cream

Put about fifteen pitted dates in a blender or grinder. Add about 1½ cups top milk and blend. When mixture is completely liquefied, pour into freezer tray and freeze. When ice cream becomes firm (but not completely frozen) beat again and refreeze. Repeat two or three times to insure smooth texture.

Pineapple Ice Cream

1 can frozen pineapple juice (undiluted)
1 papaya
2 bananas
8 soaked dried apricots
¼ cup tahini (approximately)
¼ cup sesame oil (approximately)
¼ cup honey (approximately)
3 tablespoons sunflower seeds

Liquefy and freeze to semi-solid state.

Cranberry Sherbet

1 pound cranberries
4 cups sweet apple cider
½ cup honey
1 sprig mint

Simmer cranberries in cider. Cool. In blender, blend all ingredients until smooth. Turn into ice tray of refrigerator and freeze until mushy. Beat thoroughly. Finish freezing. Serves six.

Yogurt Pineapple Sherbet

1 cup crushed pineapple with juice
1 cup yogurt

Put yogurt in freezing tray and freeze slowly to a soft mush. Remove and stir in crushed pineapple and juice. Return to freezing compartment and freeze to soft mush. Stir or beat well and freeze until solid. For variety use honey-sweetened mashed strawberries, raspberries, youngberries or other berries, finely diced peaches, apricot juice or grape juice.

Frosted Bananas

Use well-speckled ripe but firm bananas. Break in halves or thirds, according to size. Do not leave exposed to air, but prepare immediately.

Prepare a dip made of carob powder and water. Add water gradually to carob powder to a smooth consistency, not too thin, not too fudgy.

A little honey may be added to this dip if desired.

Dip bananas into carob dip, coating well all over. (Use tongs.) Then roll in grated coconut. Put each "frosted banana" in a small airtight bag and freeze.

Take out of freezer 20-30 minutes before serving.

Sunflower Seed Freeze

Put a handful of seeds, milk or water, honey, egg yolk and a few dates, raisins or figs into the blender. When it is liquefied pour it into a bowl and freeze.

Vegetable-Fruit Dessert Ices

1 quart fresh carrot juice   3 tablespoons honey
3 large oranges   (if desired)
3 medium-size bananas

Put all ingredients into blender and mix at high speed until very smooth. Pour into ice-cube trays and freeze. For smoother consistency—reblend and refreeze. Take out of freezer and refrigerate about an hour before serving.

Bean Sprout Balls

1 cup bean sprouts   1 tablespoon honey
1 cup pecans or other nuts   coconut flakes (unsweetened)
1 cup raisins

Run all ingredients through the food chopper except the honey and coconut. Add honey and mix well. Form into 1-inch balls and roll in the coconut.

Beverages

Don't introduce coffee or tea to your children, never give them a sip of yours—and they will not learn to like the taste. But do introduce them to herb teas—they are delightfully refreshing. Try mint, anis, fennel, tansey, elderberry, rose hip, licorice, alfalfa, chamomile, sarsaparilla, sassafrass, huckleberry and comfrey.

Rose Malone's Nut-Milk Shake

⅓ cup raw cashew nuts
1 cup water
3 ripe bananas
2 tablespoons food yeast
¼ teaspoon kelp

First blend nuts and water in liquifier to make milk. Then add other ingredients and blend again. Serve immediately.

Sprouted Wheat Refresher

¾ cup water
2 rounded tablespoons soaked or sprouted wheat
1 teaspoon honey

Whiz in blender. Serves one.
(Add ½ banana or 1 egg for flavor and extra nutrition.)

Cranberry Punch

Put about ½ cup of red raspberries in the blender and add:

2 cups of sweet cider
½ cup raw cranberries
1 banana
½ cup sunflower seeds

This one really packs a punch with the enzymes of the raw cranberries and the food energy, vitamin A and potassium in the banana.

Fruit Blender Drink

In the blender put the following:

1 cup raw pineapple (fresh, frozen or thawed)
3 cups water
½ cup honey
4 washed and pitted peaches

Blend, adding ice cubes until you have a thin, chilled drink. You may add sunflower seeds if you wish.

When peaches are in season, this is a great way to get lots of vitamin A while you're quenching your thirst.

Banana Shake

2 tablespoons soy powder	1 tablespoon honey
1 pint water	½ teaspoon vanilla
1 large banana	

Blend all ingredients.

Soy powder gives this beverage protein power and unsaturated fatty acids that are so good for heart and muscle health.

Dried Fruit Shake

2 tablespoons soy milk powder	honey to taste
1 pint water	blackstrap molasses
4 dates, figs, prunes or ¼ cup raisins	

Blend all ingredients.

Add sunflower seeds, sesame seeds, nuts, wheat germ, bone meal, brewer's yeast, rose hips, fresh fruits and vegetables, or whatever natural food you prefer. Besides the protein and unsaturated fatty acids of the soy, the molasses in this drink provides the iron, calcium, potassium, and 13 vitamins so vital to energy and well-being. Dried fruit provides even more zip and flavor.

Fruit Drink

In the blender:

2 cups of water	½ cup frozen strawberries
½ cup fresh pineapple chunks	Add honey to taste

Blend together and keep blender covered until just before time to drink. You can add any leftover egg yolks, plus the egg shells for added calcium and thus add nutritionally to it. Of course, you can blend in your favorite supplements.

Strawberries, besides being low in calories, are high in vitamin C and potassium. Pineapple is rich in valuable enzymes. The combination with the added nutrients of honey is a delightfully refreshing beverage.

Holiday Punch

In the blender put:

1 sliced apple
2 cups pineapple pulp and juice from the freezer

grated rind from 2 unsprayed lemons

Add hot water to blend and honey to taste, then dilute with more hot water. Shave a thin slice of lemon for the top of each glass.

Apples and pineapples are rich in important enzymes, minerals and vitamin C. The combination makes a delight-fully refreshing thirst-quenching beverage.

Carob Drink

Using carob powder instead of cocoa, make hot "choco-late" the usual way, except that you add ¼ teaspoon of pumpkin pie spice to the carob powder.

Fruit Punch

1 cup apple juice
1 cup water
1 cup grape juice

honey to taste
1 tablespoon lemon juice

Mix all ingredients together and chill well. Makes 4 servings.

The fructose in grapes supplies quick energy, and loads of minerals, especially potassium. In addition to taste, honey contributes extra energy and its own share of trace minerals.

Delicious Health Drink

16 ounces soybean milk
 1 teaspoon brewer's yeast
 1 teaspoon rose hip powder
 1 teaspoon honey
 ¼ teaspoon sea kelp

1 teaspoon blackstrap mo-lasses—rich in iron
1 teaspoon bone meal
1 or 2 teaspoons sunflower seeds

Blend all ingredients well together. For different flavors you can add walnut kernels or prunes or bananas. Recipe serves two.

This one is practically a meal. It has the complete pro-tein of the soy, amino acids, enzymes and B vitamins so plentiful in brewer's yeast, the iron of blackstrap molasses, the vitamin C of rose hip powder, the calcium, phosphorus, magnesium of bone meal, the iodine and trace minerals of sea kelp and the vitality of sunflower seeds.

Blackstrap Coffee

Try one teaspoon of blackstrap molasses, to a cup of hot water, for a cup of "black coffee" that tastes good and gives you a lift that doesn't let you down.

Home-Made Sesame Milk

1 tablespoon sobean flour	1 cup sesame seeds
3 cups water	carob or honey

Blend ½ cup of sesame seeds with one cup of water. Strain through cheese cloth. Then blend the other ½ cup of seeds with 1 cup of water and strain. Add one cup of water to the whole. Add soybean flour; carob or honey to taste.

Compare the values of sesame seed milk and cows' milk:

	100 grams Sesame Seed				
Calcium	Phosphorus	Iron	Niacin	Thiamin	Riboflavin
1125mg.	614mg.	9.5mg.	4.5mg.	.93mg.	.22mg.

	100 grams Cow's Milk				
119mg.	94mg.	0.07mg.	0.11mg.	0.37mg.	0.17mg.

Peanut Milk

In the blender put ½ cup of shelled, skinned peanuts and 2 cups of water. Blend until the nuts are mostly reduced to fine pulp. Add blackstrap molasses or honey if desired, but peanut milk is so perfectly delicious just as it is that sweeteners are unneeded. Of course add whatever supplements your family needs most. You can strain the peanut milk through a wire strainer or cheese cloth. The chunks which remain are fine to eat with a spoon.

You can get hard nuts reduced quicker if you put ¼ cup of nuts and ½ cup water in the bottom of the blender and reduce the nuts to pulp this way, then add the remainder of the water and blend it again.

Another way to make peanut milk is to take a tablespoon of homemade peanut or nut butter and stir it into a cup of warm water. This is for those who don't have blenders and who make their peanut and nut butters with a food grinder.

Almond Milk

1 cup almonds   2-4 cups water

Blend almonds with small amount of water, then add water to desired thickness. Honey may be added, but is unnecessary with fresh almonds.

Substitutes for Milk

Fill a thermos half full with wheat seeds (make sure they are not mercury treated). Add hot water and cork it. Leave overnight. Next morning grind them in your blender. Use as milk. Try this mix with wheat germ and banana for a whopping good breakfast.

Tips for Cooking Vegetables

Use as little water as possible in cooking, and save every bit of it for use in soups and gravies. Store it in a tightly covered glass jar until needed.

Use heavy stainless steel or enameled iron utensils for cooking vegetables. Have the water boiling before you add the vegetables and cover tightly; reduce heat to barely simmering. Use a large utensil so that the cover will "seal," and won't be lifted by the pressure of the steam. Cut carrots and such vegetables lengthwise and fewer nutrients will escape, especially in cooking. Cook for 6 to 8 minutes.

Never cook anything twice.

Freezing

Drop frozen vegetables into boiling water while still frozen, as vitamin C is lost during thawing.

Applesauce (raw)

All the nutrients of your apples are retained in applesauce—if it is uncooked. With this easy recipe, you can pick a few apples when you put the kettle on and have garden-fresh applesauce for dinner. If you have a whole crop of apples ready for picking, blend it into applesauce and freeze it for winter enjoyment.

4 medium-size apples   ⅛ cup lemon juice
½ cup raw honey

Wash and core apples, place all ingredients in blender and whiz.

Zesty Beets

3 cups cooked, shredded beets   ½ teaspoon sea salt
1 teaspoon onion juice   1 teaspoon honey
2 tablespoons lemon juice   ½ cup yogurt

Slip peel off the cooked beets after cooling. Shred into serving bowl.

In blender mix the yogurt, onion juice, lemon juice, honey and sea salt. Pour over beets and serve warm or chill if desired.

Mushroom Stuffed Cabbage

1 head cabbage	½ cup raw rice (brown)
3 tablespoons cold-pressed oil	1 cup boiling water
½ pound mushrooms (sliced)	1 teaspoon sea salt
½ cup chopped onions	1 cup strained tomatoes

Cover cabbage with boiling water and let stand 10 minutes to soften. Carefully remove 16 leaves. Heat 1 tablespoon of oil in a skillet and sauté the mushrooms and onions 10 minutes.

Heat another tablespoon oil in saucepan, stir in rice and cook until it is yellow. Add boiling water, cover and cook over low heat until tender and dry. Mix in the vegetables and salt. Place a heaping tablespoon of the mixture on each cabbage leaf, turn in the ends and roll up. Shred the remaining half of cabbage and spread in a casserole; arrange cabbage rolls over it. Add tomatoes and remaining oil. Cover and bake at 350°, 1 hour, removing cover the last 15 minutes. Serves 4 as a main course.

Cabbage and Nut Concoction

2 cups shredded cabbage	sea salt and paprika, as desired
½ cup chopped pecans or raw peanuts	
3 tablespoons olive or peanut oil	

Combine cabbage and nuts, olive or peanut oil and seasonings. Sauté quickly over low heat, constantly stirring.

Carrot Loaf

1½ cups grated, raw carrots	4 tablespoons soy powder
1 cup cooked brown rice	1 tablespoon nutritional yeast
¾ cup coarsely chopped, raw peanuts	1 tablespoon minced onion
2 tablespoons green pepper, chopped fine	2 beaten eggs
4 tablespoons parsley, chopped fine	2 tablespoons oil
	sea salt to taste

Mix ingredients in order given. Bake in oiled loaf pan at 350° F. for one hour. Serve with tomato sauce.

Cornmeal Mush

If your husband's parents come from the old country, this is the dish he was trying to describe to you when he said, it's hot and yellow and something like farina only much better, and you eat it with cottage cheese, sour cream, or butter.

It's a simple, economical dish made from yellow cornmeal. Use one cup for four people. Add a cup of cold water to the one cup of cornmeal and blend. Add 2 tablespoons of wheat germ to give it more pep. Add this to 3 cups of rapidly boiling salted water (1 teaspoon sea salt). Stir it as it has a tendency to stick to the pan. After it goes plop plop for a few minutes, it's ready to serve with the above-mentioned accompaniments.

If you're serving stew or any meat that has gravy, like brisket—try cornmeal mush instead of potatoes. Pour the gravy on it.

Eggplant Dish

½ cup olive oil
1 large onion (chopped)
1 large green pepper (chopped)
4 tomatoes (chopped)

1 large eggplant (diced)
½ teaspoon basil
½ teaspoon oregano
sea salt and paprika to taste

Sauté onion and pepper lightly in oil. Add tomatoes and simmer a few minutes. Add eggplant to other vegetables. Season with herbs and sea salt. Cook over medium heat until tender. Serve hot over cooked brown rice.

Sautéed Okra

½ cup oil
½ cup vinegar
1 pound fresh or frozen okra
1½ cups canned tomatoes

1 tablespoon chopped parsley
salt and pepper to taste
2-3 small onions

Wash fresh okra and trim by removing cone-shaped portions at top. Place in platter, sprinkle with vinegar and allow to stand one to two hours. Rinse thoroughly in cold water. Chop onions fine, and brown in part of oil. When browned, add tomatoes gradually. Cook two minutes and then add okra, parsley, salt, pepper, remaining olive oil, sufficient water, and two or three lemon slices if desired. Bring to a boil, then lower flame and cook slowly until ready.

Succotash

1 cup raw corn (cut off cob)
1 cup raw green lima beans
3 tablespoons shredded green pepper

1 teaspoon grated onion
oil to taste
sea salt and red crushed pepper, as desired

Combine corn, lima beans, green pepper and onion with oil and seasonings. Stir constantly over very low heat until warm.

Peas Boiled in a Jar

peas   honey
salt and pepper   mint or parsley
oil

Put the peas in a jar or little baking dish with a tight lid and add salt, pepper, 2 tablespoons oil to 1 pound peas, 1 teaspoon honey per pound, and a few mint leaves or parsley. Add no water, put on the cover, and set the jar or pot in a big kettle with boiling water coming within 2 or 3 inches below the lid of the peas. Cover the kettle and boil for ½ hour. Lift the pot of peas from the water and serve them. (Only the youngest, freshest peas can be cooked this way. Old peas will not cook tender.)

Stuffed Baked Potato

Scrub 4 medium baking potatoes; rub with oil. Bake in moderate oven (375°) one to 1¼ hours. Take slice from top of each. Scoop out inside; mash. Add oil, sea salt and hot nut milk to moisten. Beat until fluffy.

Fill shells ½ full with mashed potatoes. Combine 1 cup drained, lightly seasoned, cooked fresh peas, and 2 tablespoons chopped green onions; divide among potato shells. Pile remaining mashed potatoes atop. Return to oven (375°) 12 to 15 minutes, or until heated through and lightly browned.

Potato Chop Suey

2 medium-size potatoes in   2 raw eggs
  jackets   dash oregano
1 onion, or scallion, cut fine   2 tablespoons olive, corn or
1 chopped green pepper with   peanut oil
  seeds   sea salt and paprika as desired
2 stalks celery, chopped with
  leaves

Cut the potatoes in 1-inch slices. Sear in pan on film of oil. The slices will be raw inside, but hot. Dice these, cover and leave in pan and set aside from the heat. In another pan sear the onion, pepper and celery with seasoning desired. Be sure that these vegetables are only heated, not cooked. Mix the vegetables with the potatoes in a serving bowl and stir in the beaten eggs which serve as a sauce.

Potato Pancakes
Yield: 10-12 cakes

6 raw medium-size potatoes
1 small onion
2 eggs
⅓ cup soy milk

2 tablespoons soy flour
1 teaspoon sea salt
¼ teaspoon paprika
1 cup wheat germ

Peel and grate potatoes and onion fine. Beat in eggs and milk. Mix in wheat germ, flour, seasonings. Drop batter from spoon into hot shallow fat in a heavy skillet. Fry over low heat until each side is golden brown. Serve with applesauce, sour cream or syrup. Makes 10-12 pancakes.

Creamy Pumpkin Custard

1¾ cups cooked pumpkin (sweet potato or winter squash may be used)

¼ cup cooked brown rice
¼ cup raisins
¼ cup honey
¼ cup molasses
2 eggs
1¼ cups soy milk

1 tablespoon soy flour
⅛ teaspoon each: ginger, cinnamon, cloves
¼ teaspoon sea salt
¼ teaspoon nutmeg

Place in blender: raisins, rice, soy milk, eggs, honey, molasses, pumpkin, spices, sea salt, and soy flour. Blend until well mixed. Pour into oiled Pyrex pie pan. Place this pan in a larger pan partly filled with water. Bake at 450° for 15 minutes. Reduce heat to 350° F. Bake for 45 minutes more, or until set.

Mushrooms and Wild Rice

2 cups wild rice (soaked overnight)
2 cups diced fresh mushrooms
1 green pepper (diced)
1 diced onion

2 stalks celery with leaves
3 tablespoons soy, corn or peanut oil
sea salt and red crushed pepper, as desired

(If you don't have wild rice, use pre-cooked brown rice.)
Drain rice if any water is left. Combine with oil and seasonings. In another pan, sear quickly, over very high heat, all vegetables except mushrooms, turning constantly. When these are hot (2 minutes) remove from heat, stir in mushrooms, cover pan and let set for about 1 minute. Warm the rice in the vegetables after heating for one minute in another pan. Combine all ingredients and add some soya sauce before serving to give it an oriental flavor.

Pretty Sprouts

1 pound bean sprouts
liquid from pint of homemade
  pickled beets
2 tablespoons minced onion
2 tablespoons wheat germ

¼ cup sunflower seeds,
  coarsely chopped, or
  use sunflower meal
1 hard cooked egg, sieved or
  mashed with fork
homemade mayonnaise

Marinate sprouts all day in beet liquid. Drain well. Add remaining ingredients except egg, which will be the garnish. The beet liquid makes the sprouts a pretty color and also gives them a tangy flavor.

Sweet Potato Boats

3 large sweet potatoes
1 cup fresh cranberries
¼ cup raisins

½ cup walnuts
½ cup sesame seeds

Cook whole sweet potatoes in their jackets until just tender. Cut in half, lengthwise. Spoon out center of sweet potato halves and mash. Put remaining ingredients through the chopper. Mix this mixture with the mashed sweet potato. Fill the sweet potato with the mixture. Bake at 350° for 30 minutes.

Steamed Turnips

Pare and shred turnips. Steam only until tender. Steam them in a colander placed in a pan of boiling water with a tight lid. They should be tender in about 3 minutes. Season with a little oil, sea salt or kelp.

Zucchini in Sweet and Sour Sauce

4 sliced zucchinis
2 tablespoons oil
2 tablespoons sliced onions
¼ cup soy yogurt (home-
  made)

2 tablespoons honey
3 tablespoons apple cider
  vinegar

Sauté onions in oil. Cool. Mix yogurt, honey and vinegar and blend with zucchini and onions.

Cucumber may be substituted. Serves 6.

Rice, Noodles and Kasha

How to Make Your Own Noodles

Beat 3 eggs.

Put in bowl:

1 cup corn, rice or soy flour   3 tablespoons plain dry gelatin

Mix well. Stir in the eggs and keep stirring. It will keep getting thicker as the gelatin softens. Use a rubber scraper to form it into a ball. This noodle ball can be put into the refrigerator and sliced very thin for quick noodles. It sets very hard and is easy to slice with a sharp knife.

For noodles right away, roll the ball in arrowroot flour. Divide it into 4 pieces. Roll out each piece on arrowroot flour or use the machine. Cut into strips. For noodle sacs, cut into squares or circles, fill with a little hamburger and fold the empty half over and seal. Brown in a little oil or cook in a broth or soup. For making any of these, I prefer rolling them out by hand on a cutting board. For almost no work at all, slice them off a noodle ball.

I learned this from Freida Nusz, who wrote "Wheat and Sugar Free."

Cooking Natural Brown Rice

1 cup brown rice   2½ cups cold water
1 teaspoon sea salt

Add rice and salt to water and bring to a boil. Boil for 5 minutes. Cover tightly, turn heat very low and simmer for 45 minutes without lifting lid. Turn off heat and let set on hot burner 10 minutes. The water should be absorbed and the rice can be separated by stirring with a fork. Serves four people.

Persian-American Rice

5 cups water
2 cups brown rice
4 carrots, sliced into thin sticks, one inch long
2 fresh beets, sliced like carrots
⅓ cup raisins

¼ cup almond slices (not slivers)
2 tablespoons safflower oil
2-3 teaspoons honey
dash of onion powder, garlic powder, pepper and saffron (⅛ to ¼ teaspoon)
1 teaspoon sea salt

170

Sauté almonds in oil and cook over medium-low heat in a large saucepan for a few minutes. Watch and stir and when they begin to brown, add the raisins and lower the heat. Continue stirring and when raisins begin to become puffy, pour water into the saucepan and turn heat up to high. While waiting for water to boil, add the spices to the water. It is best to dilute saffron powder (or crumbled saffron) in a small amount of water before adding it. Add sea salt and one teaspoon honey. When water begins to boil, sprinkle rice into boiling water making sure that water continues to boil gently. Do not sprinkle rice so fast that water stops boiling. On the other hand, do not let water boil madly. Turn heat down to a simmering temperature and cover tightly. Simmer for twenty to twenty-five minutes before removing lid.

While rice is cooking, boil carrots and beets gently in a small amount of water. Try to use just enough water so that you do not need to dispose of cooking water. Cook until vegetables are tender but not limp. When rice is done, fluff gently and pour on to a large platter. Decorate the rice with carrots and beets.

Chinese Rice

(Is made with cold rice prepared the day before.)

Take 1 cup of rice and 1 egg per person. Fry 2 onions golden in 3-4 tablespoons of oil. Add the rice and fry it, while turning constantly with a wooden spoon. After 5 minutes, add the eggs which should be previously beaten with a cup of certified raw milk or nut milk and flavored with a good soy sauce like Tamari, grated nutmeg and chopped parsley. (Make sure the soy sauce you are using is made from soybeans. Many commercial brands of soy sauce are merely almond flavored salt water.) Stir again until the eggs have set. Leave for a few minutes in the oven before serving.

Chick Pea Garbanzo Puree

Bring the chick peas to the boil in cold water with onions and seasoning. Boil for about 1½ hours. (If you soak the chick peas beforehand they will take less cooking.) When tender, reduce to a puree. Fry some onion and chopped parsley separately in cold-pressed oil. Add the puree and heat for a few minutes.

Another way of serving chick peas is to drain off liquid as soon as they are cooked and toss them in some hot oil till crisp. In this way they can be served as a garnish or a snack.

Humus
(A favorite Middle Eastern dish)

Combine about one cup of pureed chick peas with four heaping tablespoons of tahini (sesame seed butter). Add ½ teaspoon sea salt, juice of 1 clove of garlic and about three tablespoons of lemon juice. (You can use your blender to get a smooth creamy consistency.) Spread on a flat platter and garnish with paprika and parsley.

Koos-Koos

I got this recipe from "Brownie's," one of my favorite New York restaurants.

2 cups bulgur wheat	1 tablespoon sea salt
⅓ cup soybean oil	¼ cup sautéed onions
1 quart consommé, stock or water	¼ cup sunflower seeds

Brown bulgur wheat in soybean oil, stirring constantly. Add consommé, salt and onions; mix thoroughly. Place in 2-quart baking dish. Cover. Bake at 375 degrees for 40 minutes. Remove from oven. Stir in sunflower seeds. Yield: 6 to 8 servings.

Cooking Buckwheat Groats

1 cup buckwheat groats (whole)	2 cups soup stock or water
1 egg	1 teaspoon salt
	chicken fat

This is my favorite method:
Combine one cup buckwheat groats with one egg and one teaspoon salt. Place in hot, heavy skillet, stirring constantly until each grain is separate and dry. While cooking, stir in a little chicken fat. If your skillet is not heavy, you may need a little oil. Add 2 cups of actively boiling water and cover tightly. Allow to steam over low flame for 30 minutes. Serve hot with gravy or with soup.

Try

Kasha-Nut Cutlets

1 tablespoon oil	1 egg (slightly beaten)
½ onion (chopped)	1 tablespoon chopped nuts or
2 cups cooked kasha	sunflower seeds

Lightly sauté onion in the oil. Add the onions to the kasha, egg and nuts or seeds. Form into patties or drop by tablespoon onto heated skillet. Sauté both sides until nicely browned.

Kasha Casserole

This is a hearty and highly nutritious casserole that, with a green salad, makes a complete meal.

Place 1 cup groats (kasha) in a bowl and pour two cups rapidly-boiling water over them. Let stand ten minutes. Meanwhile beat together:

2 eggs	½ teaspoon either sage or
3 tablespoons salad oil	thyme and sea salt to taste

Combine the soaked groats with:

1 cup diced celery	1 cup of either diced carrot
1 cup diced onion	or corn

Next pour over all the egg and seasoning mixture. Mix well, place in a baking dish, sprinkle generously with paprika and bake in a moderate oven for about 30 minutes.

Vegetable Subgum Fried Rice

3 tablespoons soy sauce	2 eggs

Mix together and add to frying pan that has 1 tablespoon heated corn oil in it. Stir till the egg is in shreds. Then add:

1 pimiento (sliced)	1 cup bean sprouts
2 green peppers (sliced about 2″ by 1″ in size)	1 cup coarsely diced celery
	1 cup sliced onions

Cook for about 5 minutes so the vegetables are still crisp.

Then add:

6 cups brown cold cooked rice

Heat thoroughly. Serve with soy sauce.

Brown Rice Salad

1 cup brown rice	¼ cup finely chopped onion
6 tablespoons oil	¼ cup chopped chives
3 tablespoons vinegar	(optional)
salt and paprika	½ cup cooked green peas or
½ teaspoon dried tarragon	string beans
¼ cup chopped parsley	

Cook rice until just tender. While still hot, add oil, vinegar, salt, paprika and tarragon to taste. Cool. Add remaining vegetables and mix well. Chill. At serving time, pile rice salad on platter in shape of a pyramid. Surround with slices of tomato and with black and pimiento-stuffed olives.

Pilaf

¼ cup oil
3 medium onions
1 cup bulgur wheat, kasha or
brown rice

3 cups chicken soup
seasonings, salt, paprika, etc.

Sauté onions and bulgur wheat in oil until golden Add chicken soup and seasonings and turn heat down. Put lid on and set timer for 45 minutes. Don't take lid off until timer rings.

Brown Rice Pilaf

A hearty, tasty, crunchy side-dish for a buffet supper, a backyard picnic or a "covered dish" party.

3 cups uncooked brown rice
6½ cups chicken broth
3 tablespoons oil
1 teaspoon ground allspice

2 sticks cinnamon
6 tablespoons chopped
almonds
¾ cup raisins

Put the rice, chicken broth, oil, allspice, cinnamon in a flat baking dish. Mix well. Cover and bake in oven (350 degrees) for 50 minutes, or until the liquid has been absorbed and the grains are separated. Stir in the almonds and raisins. Remove cinnamon sticks. Mix well and serve.

Soups

Raw Vegetable Soups

Since raw vegetables are far superior in value to cooked, try to develop skill in making raw-vegetable soups.

Put raw corn (scraped from the cob), fresh peas, cut-up celery or carrot in the blender. Whiz till it is creamy; then heat it to serving temperature and no more.

Here's a sneaky tip to make your raw soups deliciously acceptable. Sauté about two tablespoons of onion in a little oil until just golden, then blend with the other ingredients. It makes the whole soup taste like it has been cooking for hours.

Peanut Soup

(A soup that's different and hearty.)

½ cup chopped onion
2 tablespoons peanut oil
1 tablespoon rice flour
1½ teaspoons brewer's yeast

½ cup pure peanut butter (unhydrogenated)
2 cups nut milk
2 cups tomato juice

Sauté onion in oil until tender—but not brown. Add flour and brewer's yeast. Blend in peanut butter. Add milk gradually, stirring to blend. Cook and stir until mixture comes to a boil and is thickened. Add tomato juice and bring just to a boil. Garnish with minced chives, or a few chopped nuts.

Nut Soup

1 quart stock
1 cup water
2 cups nuts
2 onions

3 tablespoons oil
1 teaspoon marjoram
1 teaspoon oregano
1 tablespoon chives, minced

Gradually blend the first 7 ingredients until smooth. Heat thoroughly. Garnish with chives. Serves 6.

Gazpacho

1 clove garlic
½ small onion, sliced
1 small green pepper, seeded and sliced
3 ripe tomatoes, quartered
1 large cucumber, peeled and sliced

¼ teaspoon freshly ground black pepper
½ teaspoon basil
1 teaspoon salt
2 tablespoons olive oil
3 tablespoons wine vinegar
½ cup chilled chicken broth or ice water

Place all ingredients in container of electric blender and blend until mixed but not smooth, about three seconds. Chill until serving time. If desired, serve with toasted whole wheat croutons. This is especially good because it is uncooked so that more of the enzymes and vitamins are retained.

Avocado Soup

2 cups nut or seed milk

1 large ripe avocado (or two medium)

Mash avocado. Slowly add milk. Season to taste with herbs and spices of your choice. Add ½ teaspoon sea salt or kelp—heat just to serving temperature and no more. Pour into heated soup bowls, garnish with chopped chives, parsley, a few sunflower seeds and sprinkle with paprika.

Fruit Soup

2 cups nut milk (try cashew)
2 cups fresh fruit or berries

1 tablespoon raw honey (optional)
1 sprig mint

Blend all ingredients together until smooth. Chill. Serves 6.

Chinese Soup

2 teaspoons corn oil (cold-pressed)
½ cup sliced dark green celery
½ cup sliced fresh mushrooms

4 water chestnuts, diced
½ cup bean sprouts
½ cup diced cooked chicken
6 cups fresh chicken broth
1 egg, beaten

Heat oil in a saucepan; add celery and mushrooms and cook 2 minutes. Stir in water chestnuts, bean sprouts, chicken and broth; cook over low heat for 10 minutes. Add egg gradually, mixing steadily to prevent lumps from forming. The soup will have ribbons of egg in it. Serve immediately upon removal from heat.

Lentil Soup

1 cup (untreated) lentils
1 onion (medium size)
½ cup celery leaves
½ cup parsley

2 tablespoons soy oil
¼ teaspoon sweet basil
kelp or sea salt to taste

Wash lentils and soak 2 hours. Chop onion, celery leaves and parsley very fine. Add vegetables and soy oil to lentils. Cook in water in which they were soaked. Simmer until tender. Add seasoning and simmer 5 minutes.

Corn and Bean Soup

Add 1 beef bone to a quart of water with the following ingredients:

1 teaspoon apple cider vinegar (helps to draw the calcium out of the bone)
1 small onion
1 celery stalk, chopped
kernels from one ear of corn
½ cup pea beans or soy-
   beans which have soaked
   overnight

½ teaspoon celery salt
parsley
pinch of dill

Simmer till done.

Soybean Soup

2 cups tomatoes
1 medium chopped onion
½ cup chopped celery
½ cup diced carrots (about
   1 medium)

1¼ cups cooked soybeans,
   mashed or chopped
2 tablespoons soy flour

(Soybeans must be cooked in advance for at least an hour, or until soft. Try soaking beans overnight before cooking. A little oil added to the water before soaking helps to soften the beans.)

Cook celery, onion and carrots in 3 cups of water for about 10 minutes. Add tomatoes and mashed soybeans and heat through. Mix flour with a little cold water and stir into mixture, cooking over low heat until thickened. If desired, add your favorite seasoning. Serves 4.

Salads

Tips on preparing salads:

Never soak fruits or vegetables in water. You can lose fantastic amounts of vitamins and minerals in that way. If you have to buy produce in stores, wash it as soon as you can in very cold water. What you will use for the next meal may be shaken well, and stored in a covered dish, but the foods to be kept for a few days should be dried quickly and stored in crisper bags, tightly shut to exclude air.

Prepare salads just before serving. Keep them covered until they are eaten. Fix only enough for each meal.

You can freeze some salad vegetables. For tomatoes, cut in quarters, remove all of the white around the stem, pack in sterilized chilled jars and freeze quickly. Eat before they are completely thawed. Cucumber slices are packed in small jars, and frozen with onion slices, vinegar and all. They, too, are eaten before they are completely thawed. Peppers and pimientos are halved, all seeds and membranes removed, and packed in freezer sacks. The same goes for fresh herbs and dill. Freeze plum tomatoes whole—use in cooking.

Bean and Cabbage Salad

1½ cups cooked beans (soy, kidney or other)
¾ teaspoon kelp powder
⅓ cup mayonnaise
2 tablespoons cider vinegar
½ teaspoon paprika
2 cups shredded cabbage
½ cup chopped celery
¾ cup shredded carrots
2 tablespoons minced onion

Combine the beans, kelp, mayonnaise, vinegar and paprika. Mix in the cabbage, celery, carrots and onion. Chill. Serve on salad greens, garnish with tomato wedges and parsley.

Cabbage, Walnut and Apple Slaw

6 cups finely-shredded, dark green cabbage
½ cup coarsely chopped walnuts
1 cup coarsely chopped tart apples
¾ teaspoon sea salt

¾ teaspoon ground ginger
½ cup homemade mayonnaise
1 tablespoon apple cider vinegar
1 tablespoon pure honey

Mix together cabbage, walnuts, apples, sea salt and ginger. Place in a large glass bowl. Combine mayonnaise with vinegar and honey and pour over the slaw. Toss lightly. Chill in refrigerator and serve cold. Garnish with parsley flakes, if desired.

Pineapple Slaw

3 cups shredded cabbage
½ cup cubed pineapple

⅓ cup mayonnaise or salad dressing

Combine cabbage, pineapple and mayonnaise or salad dressing. Serves 4.

14 Vegetable Salad Bowl

1 clove garlic
1 cup spinach leaves
1 cup chopped celery
¼ cup slivered onions
1 small head chicory
1 small head lettuce
1 sliced cucumber
1 small head cauliflower (raw, broken into flowerettes)

1 head watercress (separated)
10 sliced radishes
1 bunch chopped parsley
4 sliced tomatoes
1 green pepper (cut into rings)
2 shredded carrots
French dressing

Cut garlic clove and rub bowl with it. Wash all vegetables and dry thoroughly between towels. Tear spinach, chicory and lettuce leaves. Add remaining ingredients and toss together. Add enough dressing to coat vegetables but not to soak them. Serve from salad bowl. Serves 8.

Garbanzo Salad

2 cups chopped Savoy cabbage
1 cup cooked chick peas, drained
½ cup purple, Italian onion (chopped or sliced fine)
¼ cup chopped pimiento

½ teaspoon sweet basil
sea salt
½ cup pure cider vinegar
⅓ cup olive oil
1 tablespoon mayonnaise

Combine and serve.

Harvest Salad

A colorful accompaniment to your meal, it doubles as dessert.

1½ cups red apples, peeled, cored and diced
3 tablespoons lemon juice
1½ cups celery, diced

1½ cups sun-dried unsulphured dates, chopped
¾ cup homemade mayonnaise
dash of sea salt

Combine the apples with the lemon juice. Blend the apples, celery, dates, and salt with the mayonnaise. Serve on crisp lettuce.

Mixed Root Salad with Watercress

½ cup grated carrot
½ cup grated parsnip

½ cup grated root artichokes
½ cup grated turnip

Combine with:
1 tablespoon raisins
1 tablespoon grated raw beet root

1 finely-chopped leek to taste

Arrange the different vegetables on a plate in little heaps on top of the watercress.

Carrot-Apple Salad

2 carrots
2 apples
½ cup raisins

½ cup yogurt or 2 tablespoons homemade mayonnaise for dressing

Grate carrots and apples together in a bowl. Add raisins and dressing. Stir.

Sauerkraut Salad

Rich in vitamin C, this salad goes great with meat dishes.

2 cups sauerkraut (drained)
2 cups bean sprouts (drained)
1 cup chopped onion
1 cup chopped celery

1 cup chopped green pepper
1 cup honey
½ cup apple cider vinegar
¼ cup water

Mix sauerkraut, bean sprouts, celery, onions and green pepper. Cook honey, vinegar and water for 5 minutes. Cool, then pour over the kraut mixture. Cool in refrigerator for about 24 hours before serving.

Sprout Salad

2 cups fresh sprouts   1 small minced onion
½ cup grated carrots

Blend together and dress with cold-pressed oil, pure cider vinegar, supplements and paprika. Fill lettuce cups with this mixture and serve immediately.

Raw Beet Gelatin Salad

1 carrot, raw
4 medium or 6 small fresh raw beets, cut
1 teaspoon apple cider vinegar (or lemon juice)
3 medium oranges

1 handful celery greens (2½ celery stalks)
some parsley
1 handful china peas (edible pod peas) (optional)
2 tablespoons soaked seedless raisins with juice
envelope unflavored gelatin

Put all in blender with some unsweetened pineapple juice.
In a big bowl have ready the unflavored plain gelatin. (3 tablespoons to 2 cups of hot water.) Put all in bowl and refrigerate.

Here is a recipe for a fine fruit salad:

1 envelope of gelatin
½ cup of cold fruit juice
1 cup hot fruit juice
¼ cup honey
dash of sea salt

¼ cup lemon juice
1 cup sliced bananas or pears
½ cup of rose hip mash or puree

Soften gelatin in cold fruit juice, add the hot fruit juice—apple or grape—honey and sea salt. Stir until dissolved, add lemon juice and rose hip mash. Chill until mixture is the consistency of unbeaten egg whites. Now stir in the sliced fruit and pour into molds.

Mom's Delicious Herb Salad Dressing

1 clove garlic
⅓ cup apple cider vinegar
oil (sesame, soy and wheat germ)

herbs—oregano, basil, parsley, dill or a good herb seasoning

Crush garlic into salad dressing cruet. Add ⅓ cup apple cider vinegar, combination of herbs, ⅓ cup soy oil, ⅓ cup sesame oil and 1 tablespoon wheat germ oil.
Shake well before using.

Basic Mayonnaise

1 egg	½ teaspoon sea salt
2 tablespoons fresh lemon juice	dash of cayenne
1 teaspoon honey	1 cup cold-pressed oil (soy or corn)

1. Have all ingredients at room temperature.
2. In small mixing bowl, with electric beater set at medium speed, beat egg, honey, 1 tablespoon lemon juice, salt and cayenne—until thick.
3. Add ¼ cup oil, one drop at a time, beating constantly until thick.
4. Slowly add remaining oil, a tablespoon at a time in the beginning, beating well after each addition; then adding oil in a steady stream, beating continuously until mixture reaches a thick consistency.
5. Gradually add remaining lemon juice and continue beating until thoroughly combined.
6. Refrigerate, covered, until ready to use.

Makes approximately one cup

Note: Making a good mayonnaise is easy if you remember one thing; add the oil very slowly, a drop at a time in the beginning, blending it thoroughly with the other ingredients to keep it from separating and floating on the top.

Soy Mayonnaise

For those many recipes that call for homemade mayonnaise, here's one that's easy to make.

¾ cup water	¼ cup lemon juice
¾ cup soybean powder	1 cup vegetable oil
½ teaspoon sea salt	

Stir soybean powder into oil. Add other ingredients slowly, stirring continuously.

Cashew Mayonnaise

Place in blender bowl:

½ cup raw cashews	1 cup water
1 teaspoon kelp or sea salt	garlic or onion, or herbed seasoning powder
½ teaspoon paprika	

Blend well, and slowly add 1 cup salad oil. Blend until smooth; then, with blender running, add juice of 2 lemons or 2 tablespoons cider vinegar.
Delicious with either fruit or vegetable salad.

Avocado Spread

The avocado has protein, unsaturated fats, vitamins A, B, C and E, calcium, phosphorus and iron as well as a thick skin to repel any sprays used.

1 ripe avocado, peeled and pitted
1 small yellow tomato

2 green onions, minced
1 teaspoon pure vinegar
1 teaspoon sea kelp

The quickest way to make this spread is with a potato masher or a fork, as there is hardly enough to use the blender. This spread has a cool, clean taste. You can use it as a salad dressing, a dip, or fill peppers and tomatoes with it if you live where avocados are plentiful and inexpensive.

Emerald Dressing

1 cup soy oil
⅓ cup salad vinegar
¼ cup chopped onion
¼ cup minced parsley

2 tablespoons finely-chopped green pepper
2 teaspoons honey
1 teaspoon sea salt
½ teaspoon paprika

Combine all ingredients in jar or blender. Cover and set aside for an hour. Shake 5 minutes or blend thoroughly before serving. Makes about 1½ cups of dressing. Nice with seafood or tossed green salads.

Carolyn's Eggplant Salad Dressing

Bake eggplant, peel and mash. Dice green pepper, red tomato, onion, cucumber and mix together with mashed eggplant.

Mix:
juice of 1 lemon
⅓ cup of oil
smidgeon of crushed garlic

salt and pepper
½ teaspoon raw sugar

Combine mixtures.

Yogurt Dressing

Add to ½ cup yogurt and beat slightly:

2 to 4 tablespoons lemon juice or tarragon or wine vinegar (omit if yogurt is tart)
¼ to ½ teaspoon dry mustard

½ teaspoon salt
½ to 1 teaspoon paprika
1 minced clove garlic
1 finely chopped or grated onion

Let stand in refrigerator 15 minutes before serving. Serve on head lettuce or any mixed vegetable salad. For fruit salad use yogurt without adding seasonings.

Barbecue Sauce

It's nice to be able to make your own barbecue sauce. Then you know what's in it—and no additives. This one is delicious and tangy.

1 cup tomato puree
1 large tomato
2 tablespoons cold-pressed oil
¼ cup apple cider vinegar

⅛ teaspoon cayenne
3 tablespoons honey
1 medium onion (sliced)
½ green pepper (sliced)

Mix in blender until smooth. Serve on meats, etc. Use as a basting sauce on broiled or roasted meats or chicken. Keep refrigerated.

Homemade Catsup

1 cup tomato puree (whiz 6 large plum tomatoes in blender)
¼ cup soy, sesame or safflower oil

1 tablespoon raw honey
1 tablespoon lemon juice
1 teaspoon grated onion
½ teaspoon sea salt
pinch of basil or oregano

Combine all ingredients and whiz in blender.

Yogurt French Dressing

½ cup yogurt
½ teaspoon dry mustard
½ teaspoon sea salt
2 teaspoons grated onion
2 tablespoons chopped chives

¼ cup soy oil
1 tablespoon wheat germ oil
1½ tablespoons apple cider vinegar
pinch thyme

Add mustard, salt, thyme, onion and chives to yogurt. Gradually add oils, then vinegar. Beat vigorously.

Yogurt and Cheese

Kefir is another food something like yogurt, its use dating back to Biblical times. It can be used with all kinds of milk, nut, soy, certified raw and even plain water. Because the milk need not be heated, there is no destruction of enzymes.

To make your own kefir, you need kefir grains. They cost between $5 and $10, but you never need to reorder. They last indefinitely. Order from R. A. U. Biological Laboratory, 35 Park Avenue, Blue Point, Long Island, N.Y.

All you have to do is place 1 tablespoon of kefir grains in a glass of milk, stir and leave at room temperature overnight. The next morning, drink the coagulated milk.

You should use bottled water free of chlorine and fluorides to make your kefir milk. Chlorine and fluorides are enzyme inhibitors.

Kefir Cocktail

Add a pint of water to kefir grains, two slices of lemon, two ounces of honey and a dried fig. Let stand for 24 hours. Chill for an hour and enjoy a most delightful and refreshing drink.

Make Your Own Cheese—free of fillers, free of chemicals and *fresh!*

Cottage Cheese—You will need sour milk. To make sour milk, place a bottle of certified raw milk in a pan of warm water and warm it to about body temperature—till a drop or two on your wrist feels neither hot, nor cold. Remove the cream from milk if you want skim milk cottage cheese. Place this milk in a crockery bowl and add a tablespoon of yogurt. Cover loosely with a napkin or paper towel and keep it in a warm place—on a radiator or on the back of the stove. In about 24 hours, the milk will be soured. Save about ¼ cup as a culture for your next batch.

To make cottage cheese, heat the soured milk to about 150 degrees by placing the container in warm water. When the milk has curdled, place a double thickness of cheese

185

cloth over a deep strainer set into a bowl, pour the curdled milk over it and drain. This makes a delicious cottage cheese. (Be sure to save the water which has drained off. This is the whey—rich in minerals and helpful to your intestines. Mix it with apple, grape or cranberry juice for a fine drink.)

Here is another way to make cottage cheese: Heat one quart of milk in a double boiler. When warm, add one tablespoon of lemon juice. Stir and keep heat low. When milk curdles, pour it into cheese cloth the same as above.

If you like creamed cottage cheese, add a little yogurt to it. Season with kelp, dill, parsley or paprika. Go creative with herbs!

Cream Cheese—Put a half pint of yogurt in several thicknesses of cheese cloth and let hang suspended from the faucet in your kitchen sink overnight. Make sure to place a bowl to catch the good, rich drippings, which you can drink or add to juices. In the morning you will find a lovely ball of cream cheese—tempting and delicious. Flavor it if you like with a good vegetable salt, kelp or paprika.

Soy Cheese from Soy Flour—Using 2 cups soy flour, make a paste with cold water. Add 1 quart boiling water, set on burner, stir constantly, let simmer, after it boils up, for five minutes. Take off stove, add ½ cup apple cider vinegar. Stir. Let set for 5 minutes. Pour in cheesecloth bag, squeeze.

Can be eaten as is or add chopped onion, garlic, pimiento, parsley, salt, pepper, homemade salad dressing, horseradish, chopped olives to suit taste.

Yogurt Dip

1 clove garlic	dash of vinegar (optional)
2 or 3 walnuts	1 cup thick yogurt
1 teaspoon olive oil	diced cucumber
salt and paprika	

Molasses Yogurt. Many people like to add a spoonful or two of plain, blackstrap or Barbados molasses to their yogurt. This not only gives it a rich flavor, but adds iron to supplement the mineral content in the milk.

Bake Your Own Bread

Fill the house with that wonderful yeasty fragance of home-made bread. There is no accomplishment more satisfying and no aroma more wonderful to come home to.

Helpful Hints on Baking a Good Loaf of Bread:

Assemble your equipment before you begin: a large mixing bowl, two measuring cups, a rubber spatula. If you have an electric beater, use it to develop the gluten in the flour.

Have all ingredients at room temperature.

When mixing the last portion of the flour into your dough, use only enough to assure a silky but non-sticky dough.

Oil your hands slightly before kneading.

If you use raw potato water in your bread wherever plain water is called for, you have a better chance of getting a bread that does not crumble.

To make raw potato water, put a diced potato in a measuring cup and fill with tepid water. Whiz in blender. If you don't have a blender, grate the potato instead of dicing it. Put pulp in measuring cup, fill with water and mix thoroughly.

Sprouts (wheat, rye, alfalfa) can be added to any bread dough to make a superior, moist, delicious loaf. Sprouts can be chopped, blended or used whole. Work them into the dough during the last kneading. Limit the sprouts to one cup for every 2 cups of liquid in the recipe.

Sourdough Starter

½ cup lukewarm water

1 teaspoon yeast (a natural leavening such as "Lacto Leven Lifter" is good— may be ordered by mail from Oscar Theirson, Juda, Wisc.)

Soak five minutes

Add:

½ cup warm water and enough rye flour (or other whole grain flour) to make a soft batter.

187

Place in bowl large enough to allow mixture to double in bulk.
Cover lightly and set at room temperature. Do not stir, but let
rise and fall for 24 to 36 hours, depending on sourness desired.
If you do not use at once, cover tightly and refrigerate.

Simple Sour Rye Bread

8 cups fresh whole rye flour   ½ cup sourdough starter
3 cups warm water

Mix 7 cups of flour with water and sourdough starter. Cover
and let stand in warm place overnight. Add remaining flour and
mix well. Place in oiled pans. This recipe make two large loaves.
Let rise for about a half hour. Bake at 350° for about one hour.
Be sure to retain a half cup of dough as a starter for your next
baking. Keep it in a tightly closed jar in the refrigerator.

Rye Bread

Place 2 level tablespoons yeast in cup warm water. Set aside.
In mixing bowl place:

2 cups whole wheat flour   ½ cup powdered milk
1 cup rye flour   (not instant)
2 cups warm water   2 eggs
½ cup molasses and honey   ½ cup oil
  mixed

Beat a few seconds with electric beater; add yeast.
Cover bowl with towel. Set aside in warm place until doubled
in bulk.
Add 1 tablespoon sea salt and 4 tablespoons caraway seeds.
Measure 3 cups rye flour. Gradually add flour to mixture until
it can be handled on board without excessive sticking. Knead in
remaining flour. Rye flour dough is very sticky, so moisten hands
now and then with any vegetable oil. Knead well, then shape into
2 loaves.
Place into two oiled pans. When almost doubled in bulk, or
when dough does not spring back when lightly pressed with
finger, place in oven preheated to 350°. Bake for 45 minutes.
Turn out on rack to cool.

Cornbread
(Yeast-Rising)

This recipe was developed at Fitness House—the Rodale
Press dining room.

2 packages dried yeast (¼ ounce each) or one tablespoon
1 cup tepid water
1 cup cornmeal (white or yellow)
½ cup oat flour
¼ cup soy flour
½ cup powdered skim milk
1 teaspoon sea salt
3 tablespoons honey
3 tablespoons oil
2 eggs, beaten
2 tablespoons nutritional yeast

1. Dissolve yeast in lukewarm water and allow to stand for ten minutes.

2. Combine in mixing bowl cornmeal, oat and soy flours, powdered skim milk and sea salt.

3. Add honey, oil and beaten eggs. Blend with dry ingredients.

4. Gradually add yeast mixture, blending well into other ingredients. Add nutritional yeast if desired.

5. Pour batter into a well-oiled (8 × 8) square pan. Place pan in warm area and allow to rise thirty to forty minutes. Bake in preheated oven at 350° F. for thirty to thirty-five minutes. Cool slightly (about 10 minutes), cut into squares and serve warm.

Peanut Muffins

2 eggs, separated
2 tablespoons cooking oil
½ cup chopped raw peanuts (optional)
1 tablespoon maple syrup
½ cup sifted peanut flour
½ cup wheat germ flour

Beat the whites and set aside. They should be stiff enough to hold peaks. Put the egg yolks under the beaters, add the other ingredients in order, beating well after each addition. Fold in the egg whites and pour batter in oiled muffin tins. Bake about 25 minutes at 350 degrees. Makes 6 delicious muffins.

Buckwheat Muffins

1⅓ cups buckwheat flour
⅔ cup nut flour (grind nuts in blender)
½ teaspoon sea salt
2 tablespoons wheat germ
1 teaspoon bone meal
1 tablespoon blackstrap molasses
1 tablespoon oil
3 eggs, separated (beat whites stiff)
½ cup raisins (soaked)
1 cup water (more, if necessary)

Combine ingredients, beaten egg whites last (folded in carefully). Bake 20 minutes at 425°. Makes 12 muffins.

Rice Muffins

3 eggs, separated
2 tablespoons maple syrup
1 cup soy milk
1 teaspoon sea kelp

½ cup almonds
2 tablespoons cooking oil
1 cup brown rice flour
1 cup rice polishings

Beat the egg whites until stiff and set aside. Combine the other ingredients and beat until very light. Fold in egg whites, pour the batter in oiled muffin tins and bake about 25 minutes at 400 degrees. Makes 12 muffins.

A Crunchy Biscuit with Whole Sesame Seeds

1 cup sesame seeds
4 cups buckwheat flour
1 teaspoon sea salt

4 tablespoons soy or corn oil
2 cups water
cinnamon

Make firm dough, roll in shape of sausage and cut in slices. Fry in hot oil.

Peanut Corn Sticks

1 cup yellow cornmeal   ½ cup boiling water

Pour the boiling water over the cornmeal, blend and cool. Add the following ingredients to the cornmeal mixture:

1 teaspoon sea kelp
1 egg yolk
1 tablespoon honey
1 rounded tablespoon peanut butter

1 rounded tablespoon brown rice flour
½ cup soy milk

Blend together and fold in 1 stiffly beaten egg white. Have the oven preheated to 425° and have the oiled corn-stick pan in it, very hot. Fill it with the mixture and bake until done, about 10 to 12 minutes. This recipe fills the corn-stick pan just once, but you can double or triple it for extra batches.

Peanut Butter

Ideally, peanut butter should be ground raw peanuts with nothing added. Such peanut butter is available at health food stores and at some supermarkets. Read the label carefully. Most commercial peanut butters have hydrogenated fats added to them. These are oils which have been treated chemically with hydrogen so that they become solid at room temperature even though they are vegetable oils which are, in their natural state, liquid at room temperature.

The solid, hydrogenated oils keep the peanut butter from separating. They also convert the good, unsaturated fats of the natural peanut oil into an unhealthful, hard-to-digest saturated fat.

If you can't find natural peanut butter in you own town, try making your own. You'll enjoy the wonderful taste.

Homemade Nut Butters

Peanut: Grind peanuts or crush with rolling pin till very fine. Add enough oil to make spreadable. Keep refrigerated.

Almond, walnut, cashew or brazil nut butters are made the same way but these nuts may not need any additional oil.

Have you ever tried soybeans? They have a marvelous nutlike flavor.

You can utilize the marvelous values of the soybeans on your snack tray with this great recipe.

Soy Butter

Mix ¼ cup soybean oil into ¾ cup soybean powder. This is the basic spread—somewhat the consistency of peanut butter. Now go creative. Mix or match with these flavor enhancers:

½ teaspoon onion, celery or garlic salt or herb seasoning
½ cup chopped nuts or soy granules

½ cup chopped sunflower, sesame or pumpkin seeds
¾ cup dark molasses (blackstrap or sorghum)
½ cup wheat germ flakes

Homemade Cashew Butter

A delicious spread for pancakes, toast or stuffed into celery.

Pour 1 cup raw cashew bits into the blender with 1 tablespoon sesame seeds. Blend. Pour mixture into a mixing bowl and mash lumps with a tablespoon. Spoon into a glass container with a screw top.

Add ⅓ cup soy oil and mix thorougly. Refrigerate at least overnight before serving. For variation add ½ cup fresh, crushed, unsweetened pineapple and ¼ cup raw honey.

Sugarless Jelly

3 to 4 quarts blueberries (or   3 or 4 cups apple cider (for
    any fruit in season)   sweeter taste add more)

Place washed blueberries in pan on low heat with cover till blueberries cook well. Boil till thickened slightly. Add apple cider, continue boiling without cover, add pectin or sur-jell. Continue boiling until slightly thickened.

Pack in hot jars. Process in hot water bath for 5 minutes. Seal tightly for winter.

Sunglow Spread

A nice change from peanut butter. Keep it in the refrigerator. Let the children help themselves. It's great on sliced apples.

1 cup wheat germ   1 cup sunflower seed meal
2 cups honey   1 cup pumpkin seed meal

Shake dry ingredients in wide-mouth Mason jar to distribute evenly. Cut in honey with knife, or tighten cap and turn jar until honey is absorbed thoroughly.

The Percentage of the Mineral Content of Nuts Is Given in the Following Chart

	Phosphorus	Potassium	Calcium	Magnesium	Sodium	Chlorine	Iron	Sulfur	Zinc	Manganese	Copper
Almond	.475	.759	.254	.252	.026	.020	.0044	.150	.0019	.0008	.0015
Brazil	.602	.601	.124	.225	.020	.081	.0028	.198	....	....	.0014
Butternut	....	....	....	....	....	....	.0068	....	....	....	.0012
Cashew	.480	....	.048	....	....	....	....	....	....	....	....
Chestnut	.093	.560	.034	.051	.065	.006	.0070	.068	.0004	.0031	.0078
Coconut	.191	.693	.043	.077	.053	.225	.0036	.076	.0010	....	....
Hazlenut	.354	.618	.287	.140	.019	.067	.0041	.198	.0010	....	.0012
Hickory nut	.370	....	....	.160	....	....	.0029	....	....	....	.0014
Macadamia	.240	....	.053	....	....	....	.0020	....	....	....	....
Peanut	.392	.614	.080	.167	.039	.041	.0019	.226	.0016	.0020	.0009
Pecan	.335	.332	.089	.152	....	.050	.0026	.113	....	.0043	.0010
Pistachio	....	....	....	....	....	....	.0079	....	....	.0007	.0012
Walnut, black	.091	.675	.071	.098	....	....	.0060	....	....	.0033	.0032
Walnut, English ...	.038	.332	.089	.134	.023	.036	.0021	.146	.0020	.0018	.0011

The Food Value of Nuts

	Percentage of			Calories
	Carbohydrate	Protein	Fat	Per Pound
Acorn	57.10	6.65	5.0	1909
Almond	4.3	20.5	16.0	3030
Beechnut	13.2	21.9	57.4	2846
Brazil Nut	4.1	13.8	61.5	3013
Butternut	3.5	27.9	61.2	3165
Cashew	29.4	21.6	39.0	2866
Chestnut	36.6	2.3	2.7	1806
Coconut	27.9	5.7	50.6	2760
Filbert	9.3	14.9	65.6	3288
Hickory Nuts	11.4	15.4	67.4	3342
Lichee	78.0	2.9	.80	1539
Macadamia Nuts	8.2	8.6	73.0	3507
Peanuts	8.6	28.1	49.0	2645
Pecans	3.9	9.4	73.0	3539
Pine Nuts	6.9	33.9	49.4	3174
Pistachio	16.3	22.3	54.0	2996
Walnut, Black	10.20	27.6	56.3	3180
Walnut, English	5.0	12.5	51.5	3326

INDEX

INDEX

Abdominal pains, 55, 57
Absorption, 73, 83
Additives, 12, 34–35, 62, 82
Adulterated food products, 35, 82
Agricultural Handbook of the Composition of Foods, The, 73
Airola, Dr. Paavo, 81, 82, 87
Allergies, 37, 48, 55
Aluminum, 14
American Journal of Obstetrics and Gynecology, 30
Amino acids, 37, 87
Antihistamine, 55
Apples, 38, 39, 106
Art of Cooking with Rose Hips, The, 86
Arthritis, 12, 72
Artificial fertilizers, 85
Ascorbic acid, 97
Aspartic acid, 87

Baby food: 34–39
   Dab cookery, 37–39
   Make your own, 35
   Salt and hypertension, 35–36
Bake Your Own Bread, 187–190
Baking Hints, 145

Banana, 39, 90
   (see also recipes)
B complex, 31, 56, 58, 61, 63, 72–73, 78, 82, 83, 84, 87, 106
Beans:
   cranberry, 23
   fava, 23
   Italian green, 117
   lima, 23
   marrow, 23
   mung, 21, 23
   snap, 32
   soy, 17, 22–23, 32, 56
Beriberi, 56–57, 59
BEVERAGES, 109
   Almond Milk, 163
   Apple-Pineapple Punch, 109–110
   Banana Yeast Shake, 31, 160
   Blackstrap Coffee, 162
   Carob Drink, 161
   Cranberry Punch, 159
   Delicious Health Drink, 161–162
   Dried Fruit Shake, 160
   Fresh Cantaloupe Shake, 119
   Fruit Blender Drink, 159–160
   Fruit Drink, 160
   Fruit Punch, 161
   Holiday Punch, 161

197

BEVERAGES *(Continued)*
  Homemade Sesame Milk, 162
  Jerusalem Artichoke Flip, 118
  Kefir Cocktail, 185
  Papaya Punch, 109
  Peanut Milk, 162
  Rose Malone's Nut Milk Shake, 159
  Soya Shake, 93
  Substitutes for milk, 163
  Sprouted Wheat Refresher, 159
BHA, 13, 52
BHT, 13, 52
Bioflavonoids, 29–30, 96
Bircher-Benner Clinic, 142
Blackstrap molasses, 33, 90
Blood sugar, 58, 62, 63
Brain damage, 34
Brains, 25, 122
  good for heart, 77
  how to sneak into diet, 78
  smart nutrition in, 77
  (see also meat recipes)
Bread, 56, 58, 85, 92, 117, 132, 143–144
  additives, 13
  enrichment fiasco, 18, 57
  homemade, 187
  (see also BREAD recipes)
BREADS, CRACKERS, CEREALS AND NUTS
  Banana Nut Loaf, 146
  Barley Pancakes, 143
  Buckwheat (Kasha) Delight, 142
  Buckwheat Muffins, 189
  Canape Crackers, 107
  Cooking Buckwheat Groats, 172
  Cornbread, 188–189
  Corn Chapatties, 65–66
  Corn Chips, 111
  Corn Crisp Crackers, 107
  Cornmeal Crackers, 107
  Cornmeal Mush, 165–166
  Crunchy Biscuit with Sesame Seeds, 190
  French Toast, 143–144
  French Toasted Cheese Sandwich, 117
  Get Up and Go Pancakes, 64–65
  Golden Millet, 141
  Granola Mix, 141–142
  Helpful Hints on Baking a Good Loaf of Bread, 187
  How to Make Dry-Roasted Soy Nuts, 110–111
  Kasha-Nut Cutlets, 172
  Oatmeal Crackers, 108
  Old Fashioned Buckwheat Pancakes, 65
  Old Soak Powerhouse Cereal, 141
  Peanut Corn Sticks, 190
  Polynesian Muffins, 65
  Rice Muffins, 190
  Rye Bread, 188
  Simple Sour Rye Bread, 188
  Sour Dough Starter, 187–188
  Soy-Corn Waffles, 143
  Soy nuts, dry roasted, 110–111
  Wheat Germ Pancakes, 66
Brin, Dr. Myron, 60
British Medical Journal, The, 42
Brody, Dr. Leopold, 84
Brownie's Restaurant, 147
Bruch, Dr. Hilda, 41

Calcium, 16, 17, 21, 50, 61, 74, 98
Calcium pantothenate, 55
California Youth Authority, 50
Calorie counting, 112, 114–116
Candy bar syndrome, 44
Capillary walls, 29
Carbohydrates, 21, 31
Cardiac necroses, 101
Carob:

flour, 13
powder, 51, 62, 98
(see recipes)
CASSEROLES
Brown Rice Pilaf, 174
Chinese Rice, 171
Chow Mein, 92
Garden of Eden Casserole, 126
Kasha Casserole, 173
Koos-Koos, 172
Oriental Rice, 116
Persian American Rice, 170–171
Pilaf, 174
Vegetable Subgum Fried Rice, 173
Cavities, 12, 121
Center for the Biology of the Natural System, University of Washington, St. Louis, Mo., 37
Cheraskin, Dr. E., 29, 61
Chlorophyll, 22
Choate, Robert B., Jr., 51–52
Choline, 31, 32, 77
Clark, Dr. J. W., 61
Cleft Palate, 32
Clover, 23
Coconut (unsweetened), 13
(see also recipes)
Collagen, 97
Coloring agents, 35
Colostrum, 31
Committee on Foods and Nutrition of The National Research Council, 60
Commoner, Dr. Barry, 37
Compte, Rendue Société de Biologie, 63
Congenital anomalies, 32
CONFECTIONS
Ambrosia Cream, 109
Apple Rice Betty, 151
Bean Sprout Balls, 158
Bone Meal Cookies, 98
Cantaloupe Sherbet, 156
Carob Brownies, 147
Carob Confection, 103

Carob Honey Cake, 146
Carolyn's Apple Cake, 145
Carrot and Nut Cake, 149
Carrot Nut Torte, 117
Coconut Banana Meringue Pie, 108
Coconut Mousse, 152
Cranberry Sherbet, 157
Creamy Pumpkin Custard, 168
Date Ice Cream, 156–157
Date Torte, 149
Frosted Bananas, 157
Fruit Candies, 153–154
Hi-Pro-Lo-Calorie Peach Whip, 118
No-Bake, No Sugar Fruit Pie, 150
Non-Wheat Pastry, 150
Peach Rice Betty, 108–109
Peanut Raisin Cookies, 148
Pineapple Ice Cream, 157
Pineapple Nut Torte, 150
Pineapple Porcupines, 103
Pineapple Pudding, 151–152
Popcorn Balls, 153
Potato Carob Bon-Bons, 154
Pumpkin Ice Cream, 156
Pumpkin Seed Candy, 106
Raspberry Ice Cream, 155–156
Raspberry Supreme, 151
Roll-ups, 154
Sesame Seed Candies, 105
Sesame Strips, 147
Sesame Taffy, 105–106
Sesame Treats, 153
Soy Walnut Cookies, 148
Soy Whipped Cream, 152
Strawberry Honey Ice Cream, 156
Sunflower Date Loaf Cake, 146
Sunflower Seed Candies, 105
Sunflower Seed Freeze, 158
Sweet Potato Almond Crustless Pie, 150–151
Tahini Cookies, 148
Tidbits, 105

CONFECTIONS *(Continued)*
  Vanilla Ice Cream, 155
  Vanilla Rice Custard, 151
  Vegetable-Fruit Dessert Ices, 158
  Yogurt-Fruit Dessert, 152
  Yogurt Pineapple Sherbet, 157
Copper, 37
Cornell University, 52
Cornmeal (see recipes)
Coronary, 11
Cornstarch, 37
Crackers (see recipes)
Cystitis, 12

Dab Cookery, 37–38
Dabs, apricot, 38
Dabs, chicken liver, 38
Dahl, Dr. Lewis K., 35–36
Davis, Adelle, 15–16, 82
DDT, 113
Deficiencies, 18, 88–99
Department of Educational Psychology at Columbia University, 60
Depression, 54–70, 71
Dewey, Governor, 22
Diarrhea, 57, 60
Diet and Disease, 61
Disposition, 17, 54–70
Division of Adolescent Psychiatry, Children's Hospital, Washington, D.C., 43
Dry skim milk, 15

Eat Fat and Grow Slim, 115
Eggs, 45, 92, 97, 102, 116
  fertile, 63–64, 98
  how to prepare, 64
  yolk, 87
  (see also EGGS AND CHEESE)

EGGS AND CHEESE
  Brains with Scrambled Eggs, 78–79
  Cottage Cheese, 185–186
  Cream Cheese, 186
  Egg Croquettes, 65
  Egg Foo Yung, 119, 144
  Eggs in the Shell, 63–64
  Egg Sauce with Brains, 79
  Gourmet Eggs, 63
  Protein Energy Omelet, 144
  Scrambled Eggs and Peppers, 64
  Soy Cheese from Soy Flour, 186
Eijkman, Dr. Christian, 59
Elwood, Catharyn, 24
Encyclopedia of Sex Practice, The, 87
Enzymes, 11, 17, 18, 21, 44, 58, 62, 73, 74, 112, 119, 185
Estrogen, 81
Exercise, 100–101, 102, 116

Fats, 16, 21, 44, 58, 95, 115
Feel Like A Million, 24
Fenugreek, 23, 94
Fetus, fatality of, 32
Filling, 136
Fish liver oil, 33, 96, 98
FISH RECIPES
  Baked Herring and Potato, 86
  Chopped Herring, 139
  Easy Fish Chowder, 138
  Flounder with Mushroom Sauce, 139
  Halibu Pilaf, 139
  Mrs. Bunn's Swordfish Banana Bake, 140
  Onion-Apple Stuffed Cod, 138
  Salmon Loaf, 139–140
Fitness House, 149
Flour:

bleached white, 13, 44, 62, 73
carob, 13
nutrition in, 17–18, 56
soy, 13
whole wheat, 13
Flourides, 185
Flourine, 74
Food value of nuts, 194
Fruit, citrus, organically grown, 30, 45
(see also FRUIT recipes)
FRUITS
Apple Muesli, 142
Applesauce, raw, 164
Fig Muesli, 143
Fruit Candies, 153–154

Gall bladder, 17
George Washington School of Medicine, 43
Gordon, Jean, 86
Greenberg, Elsa, S. Ph.D., 43

Hamburger, 122
How to sneak nutrients into, 25–27
Halvah, 75
and sex, 87
Harrell, Ruth F., 60
Heart abnormalities, 32, 55
Helix High School, 50
Hemorrhage, 32, 97
Herb seasonings, 44, 102
Higuchi, M., 86
Hinds, Judith R., 37, 38
Hoffer, Dr. Abraham, 56, 57
Honey, 13, 39, 87, 105, 106
How To Help Your Child Lose Weight, 45
How to Make Your Own Noodles, 170
Humus, 75, 172

Hurd, Dr. Frank, 155
Hypertension, 31, 35
genetic predisposition to, 36
Hypoglycemia, 44, 115
Hypothalamus, 34

Ice Cream and Other Frozen Desserts, 154–158
Importance of Overweight, The, 41
Infertility, 84
Insecticides, 85, 118
Iodine, 82, 83
Iron, 21, 37, 50
Irritability, (see Disposition)

Kale, 33
Kelp, 13, 82, 83, 134
Kernicterus, 32–33
Keys, Professor Ancel, 73
Kidneys, 25, 32, 56, 93
Kreplach, 26
Kugels, 16

Laboratory of Physical Hygiene of The University of Minnesota, 73
Larsen, Mrs. Gena, 50–51
Latham, Dr. Michael, 52
Lawson, Ray N., M.D., 114
Lead poisoning, 73
Lecithin, 115
Legumes, 102
Lentils, 23
Let's Have Healthy Children, 15
Linoleic acid, 72
Liver, 25, 32, 33, 56, 83, 84, 87, 90, 92, 98, 102
desiccated, 61, 93
(see also meat recipes)

Lollipops, 40
Low back syndrome, 12
Lowenberg, Miriam E., 59–60
Luhby, Dr. W. Leonard, 32

Macharness, Dr. Richard, 115
Mack, Dr. Pauline Beery, 50
Magnesium, 61, 73, 74, 90
Maraschino cherries, 13
Mason, Gussie, 45
Mayer, Dr. Jean, 43
McCay, Dr. Clive M., 22
McGovern Senate Investigating
  Committee, 36
MEATS
  Beef Heart Chow, 46
  Beef Liver Creole, 133
  Blender Meat Loaf, 127
  Brain Fritters, 79
  Brains with Egg Sauce, 79
  Brains with Scrambled Eggs,
    78–79
  Breast of Lamb, 131
  Chicken Hawaiian, 124–125
  Chicken Pilaf, 110
  Chopped Liver, 106, 133
  Crunchy Baked Chicken,
    125
  Fried Calves' Brains, 78
  Fried Sweetbreads, 136
  Health-Full Chop Suey, 129
  Karnatzlach, 96
  Lamb on Brown Rice, 130–
    131
  Liver Delight, 134
  Liver (for people who don't
    like liver), 134
  Liver Patties, 110
  Liver Veal Loaf, 135
  Lung and Beef Stew, 135
  Meat Balls, Millet and
    Mushroom Gravy, 128
  Meatloaf, 127
  Piquant Lung and Heart,
    133
  Pitchah-An Old World Fa-
    vorite, 131–132
  Polynesian Pot Roast, 128–
    129
  Raw Liver Pattie, 135
  Rice and Meat Sauce, 26–27
  Ruthie's "Hearty" Veal Stew,
    137
  Sauteed Sweetbreads with
    Mushrooms, 136
  Spanish Brown Rice and
    Meat, 128
  Stuffed Milt, 136
  Sukiyaki, 129–130
  Sweet and Sour Chicken,
    124
  Sweet and Sour Heart, 94
  Yogurt Beef Stroganoff, 130
Medical Research Center,
  Brookhaven National Lab-
  oratory, 36
Megaloblastic anemia, 32
Memory, lapses of, 91, 93
Menstrual cramps, 16
Mental ability,
  increased by thiamine,
  60–61
Mental health, 17
Mental retardation, 32
Mercury poisons, 24
Metabolic disturbances, 18
Methionine, 74
Millet, 23
Mineral Content of Nuts, 193
Minerals, 11, 17, 21, 44, 49,
  58, 63, 73, 74, 123
Miracle Foods, 21
Monello, L., 42
Monosodium glutamate, 34–35
Morale vitamin, 91
Moss, Senator Frank, 51

Nader Ralph, 35, 36
Necrotic tissue, 101
Neurasthemia, 57
Newer Methods of Nutritional
  Biochemistry, 60
New York Medical College, 32
Niacin, 21, 31, 56, 58, 72, 73
  and mental health, 56–57

signs of deficiency, 57, 93, 94

Night blindness, 57

Nitrates, 86, 87
dangers of, 35, 37, 95, 96

Noodles How to Make Your Own, 170

Nusz, Frieda, 75, 98

Nuts, food value of, 194
mineral content of, 193

Oatmeal, 102

Oats, 21

Obesity, 31, 40–47

Oldfield, Dr. M. J., 42

Olney, Dr. John, 34, 35

Organ meats, 25

Overweight in children, 40–47
psychological effects, 40, 42–43
what can a mother do, 44–47

Oxygen and Enzymes, 62

Pablum, 42

Pantothenic acid, 21, 55, 56, 84

Parsley, 23

Parties, what to serve, 104–111

Pauling, Dr. Linus, 97

Peanut butter, 13, 93, 190

Peas
chick, 23
green, 23

Pectin, 73

Pellagra, 56, 93

Pennsylvania State Department of Health, 50

Phosphorus, 21, 74

Pituitary, 83, 84

Polly seeds, 71–76

Polyneuritis, 59

Pories, Dr. Walter, 73

Potassium, 21, 101, 102

Prasad, Dr. A. A., 84

Pregnancy, 28–33, 60
complications of, 31, 32
erythroblastosis fetalis, 29
miscarriage, 72

nausea during, 28, 30, 31
neonatal mortality, 29
pre-eclampsia, 31
Rh incompatibility, 30
spontaneous abortion, 28, 32
toxemia, 28, 31, 32

Preservatives, 35, 74, 86

Prevention, 123

Prioreschi, Dr. P., 101

Protein, 16, 20, 21, 27, 31, 35, 37, 44, 52, 58, 62, 73–74, 75, 77, 84, 90

Puddings, 16

Purdue University Opinion Panel, 50

Pyridoxine, 21, 31

Pyroceram, 14

Radioactive strontium, 73

Reducing plan, 46–47

Respiratory failure, 36–37

Retarded growth, 32

Riboflavin, 16, 21, 50, 72, 73, 92, 93

Riboullearo, Dr., 63

Rice, 13, 26–27, 38, 59, 60, 91, 123
natural brown, 24, 26–27, 59, 82, 83, 123
(see also CASSEROLES)

Rice Noodles and Kasha, 170

Ringsdorf, Dr. W. M., 61

Rodale Books, 61

Rose Hips, 86, 87, 97, 98

Russians, 71, 73, 74–75

Rutgers University College of Agriculture and Environmental Science, 49

Rye, 14, 23, 94

Safflower oil, 84

SALADS AND SALAD DRESSINGS
Bean and Cabbage Salad, 178

SALADS AND SALAD DRESSINGS *(Continued)*
Brown Rice Salad, 173
Cabbage, Walnut and Apple Slaw, 179
Carolyn's Eggplant Salad Dressing, 183
Carrot-Apple Salad, 180
Chicken and Almond Salad, 125
Chinese Chicken Salad, 125
Dark Green and Orange Salad, 95
Emerald Dressing, 183
Fruit Salad, 181
Garbanzo, 179
Harvest Salad, 180
Jerusalem Artichoke Salad, 118
Mayonnaise, 182
  basic, 182
  cashew, 182
  soy, 182
Minted French Dressing, 153
Mixed Root Salad with Watercress, 180
Mom's Delicious Herb Salad Dressing, 181
Pineapple Slaw, 179
Raw Beet Gelatin Salad, 181
Sauerkraut Salad, 180
Sparkling Chicken Salad, 126
Sprout Salad, 181
Strawberry Filled Avocados, 153
14 Vegetable Salad Bowl, 179
Waldorf Salad, 44
Yogurt Dressing, 183
Yogurt French Dressing, 184
Salt, 35–36, 44, 101–102
  sea, 13, 116
  kelp as substitute for, 13, 83, 116, 134
Saskatchewan's Department of Public Health, 56

SAUCES, SPREADS AND DIPS
Avocado Spread, 183
Barbecue Sauce, 184
Chicken Pecan Spread, 119
Egg Sauce, 79
Get Smart Appetizer, 78
Homemade Cashew Butter, 191
Homemade Catsup, 184
Homemade Nut Butters, 191
Mushroom Sauce, 139
Peanut Butter, 190
Rice and Meat Sauce, 26
Soy Butter, 191
Sugarless Jelly, 192
Sunglow Spread, 192
Yogurt Dig, 186
Schizophrenia, 56, 57, 93
School of Nutrition, Cornell University, 22
Scurvy, 57
Seed milk, 75
Seeds, 22, 102, 123
  alfalfa, 14, 22, 23, 94
  barley, 23, 94
  chia, 23
  chick peas, 23
  clover, 23
  corn, 23, 94
  cranberry, 23
  fava bean, 23
  fenugreek, 23, 94
  lentils, 23
  lima bean, 23
  marrow beans, 23
  millet, 23
  mung bean, 14, 94
  mustard, 23
  oat, 14, 23, 94
  parsley, 23
  pumpkin, 13, 75, 85, 123
  radish, 23
  rye, 14, 23, 94
  sesame, 13, 23, 75, 84, 85, 87, 123, 133, 134
  soy bean, 14, 21
  sunflower (see Sunflower seeds)

wheat, 14, 23
Senate consumer subcommittee, 51
Sesame oil, 13
  (see recipes)
Sex and Nutrition, 81
Sex life, how to change, 80–88
Shortening, 13
Shute, Dr. Evan, 32
Sinclair, Dr. Hugh, 72
Skin, 72, 92, 116
Smith, Dr. Harvey, 114
Smokers, cut habit with polly seeds, 71
Snacks, 62
  for children, 12–13, 44
  for heart health, 100–103
  for weight watchers, 44
Sodium, 101–102
Sodium chloride, 101
Sodium nitrate, 37
Soil, Grass and Cancer, 85
SOUPS
  Avocado Soup, 176
  Chick Pea Garbanzo Puree, 171
  Corn and Bean Soup, 177
  Lentil Soup, 177
  Chinese Soup, 176
  Fruit Soup, 176
  Gazpacho, 176
  Nut Soup, 175
  Peanut Soup, 175
  Raw Vegetable Soups, 175
  Rose Hip Soup, 86
  Soybean Soup, 177
Soybeans, 23, 32, 33
  (see Beans and recipes)
Soy flour, 13, 50, 82, 92, 134
Soy powder, 15, 17, 63, 92
Spindler, Dr. Evelyn, 49
Sprouts, 21–24, 45, 92, 94, 187
  alfalfa, 22, 23, 24, 33, 187
  barley, 21, 23
  corn, 21
  mung bean, 21, 23
  rye, 187
  soybean, 21, 23

wheat, 21, 187
Stainless steel, 14
Sugar, 16, 35, 39, 44, 52, 92, 94
  date, 13, 87
  raw, 13, 123
  refined, 13, 62, 73, 122–123
Sunflower seeds, 13, 24, 71–76, 84, 85, 90, 93, 123
  source of unsaturated fatty acids, 72
Sweetbreads, 77
Synthetic sweeteners, 13

Tahini, 75
Tapioca, 37
Teens, 48–53
  food choices, 49
  nutrition and delinquency, 48
  poor eating habits, 41
Teflon, 14
Ten Talents, 155
Testosterone, 81
Thiamine, 30, 31, 50, 58–61, 72, 73, 91, 92
Thyroid, 82, 83
Tidbits, 105
Tips for Cooking Vegetables, 164–169
Tobacco, 87, 92, 97
Tocopherols, 72
Tranquilizers, 90
Treats, 108

University of Alabama, Department of Oral Medicine, 29
Unsaturated fats, 17
  fatty acids, 72
U.S. Department of Agriculture, 49
U.S. Naval Medical Research Unit, 84

Vanilla, 16, 45
VEGETABLES
Almost Raw Pumpkin, 119
Baked Jerusalem Artichoke Hash, 117
Broiled Jerusalem Artichokes, 117
Broiled Onions, 45
Brown Rice and Carrot Patties, 63
Cabbage and Nut Concoction, 165
Cabbage with Yogurt, 33
Carrot Loaf, 165
Chick Pea Garbanzo Puree, 171
Cooking Natural Brown Rice, 170
Eggplant Dish, 166
"French Fries," 116, 117
Mushrooms and Wild Rice, 168
Mushroom Stuffed Cabbage, 165
Peas Boiled in a Jar, 167
Peppers and Scrambled Eggs, 64
Potato Chop Suey, 167
Potato Pancakes, 168
Pretty Sprouts, 169
Red Cabbage and Mung Bean Sprouts Saute, 45
Sauteed Okra, 166
Soybean Chili, 127
Sprouted Soybean Curry, 24
Steamed Turnips, 169
Stuffed Baked Potatoes, 167
Succotash, 166–167
Sweet Potato Boats, 169
Zesty Beets, 164
Zucchini in Sweet and Sour Sauce, 169
Vitamin Charts, 66–69, 76, 193, 194
Vitamins, 11, 16, 17, 21, 22, 27, 30, 31, 49, 99, 123
A, 21, 50, 57, 63, 73, 84, 87, 95, 96, 114
B1, 30, 31, 56, 58, 59, 82, 83, 91, 92
B2, 16, 21, 92, 93
B3, 57, 93
B6, 30, 31, 90
C, 17, 20, 21, 29, 30, 50, 56, 86, 87, 96, 97
D, 17, 63, 74
E, 21, 27, 32, 63, 72, 81, 83, 84
K, 22, 63
deficiencies of, 33
P, 96, 97
Voison, Dr. Andre, 85

Walters, Dr. J. D., 94
Washington University School of Medicine, 34
Weiss Memorial Hospital Bulletin, 84
Werkman, Dr. Frederick, 43
Wheat and Sugar Free, 75, 98, 170
Wheat germ, 13, 17–18, 50, 56, 61, 62, 83, 91, 92, 93, 98, 122, 123
how to sneak it in, 18–19
oil, 13, 83, 84, 98
World Congress of Fertility and Sterility, 84
World War II, 22

Yeast, 13, 62, 102, 123, 134
Brewer's, 32, 58, 61, 83, 84, 90, 92, 93
how to sneak it, 56, 58
nutritional, 58, 91, 98
plant cells, 57, 58
Yogurt, 123, 185, 186
molasses, 186
(see also recipes)

Zinc, 73, 84, 85